TRIGGER POINTS

1. *The only thing we can depend on is unpredictability.*
2. *Our economic output is slowing down — and our standard of living isn't rising as fast as it used to.*
3. *We'll have a high rate of chronic unemployment for some time to come.*
4. *The mass market is splitting apart and, more than ever, the customer is the ultimate ruler.*
5. *An outside-in strategy is the only sensible option.*
6. *Raise productivity at least one and a half times higher than the real interest rate.*
7. *Beat your competition by 10 percent.*
8. *Make decisions three times faster, implement them faster — and make sure they are economically reversible.*
9. *Shoot for zero turnover of your real, genuine 24-carat talent.*

ACTION TOOLS

1. *Pyramid thinking*
2. *Directed brainstorming*
3. *Razor blade reading and clue management*
4. *Gap analysis*
5. *Action proposals: the task force approach*

TRIGGER POINTS

TRIGGER POINTS

How to Make Decisions Three Times Faster, Innovate Smarter, and Beat Your Competition by Ten Percent (It Ain't Easy!)

MICHAEL J. KAMI

McGRAW-HILL BOOK COMPANY

New York St. Louis San Francisco Auckland Bogotá Hamburg London Madrid Mexico Milan Montreal New Delhi Panama Paris São Paulo Singapore Sydney Tokyo Toronto

Library of Congress Cataloging-in-Publication Data

Kami, Michael J.,
Trigger points: how to make decisions three times faster, innovate smarter, and beat your competition by ten percent (it ain't easy!) / Michael J. Kami.
p. cm.
Bibliography: p.
Includes index.
ISBN 0-07-033219-3
1. Success in business. I. Title.
HF5386.K154 1988
650.1—dc19

1234567890 DOC/DOC 89321098

ISBN 0-07-033219-3

The editors for this book were Martha Jewett and Galen H. Fleck, the designer was Naomi Auerbach, and the production supervisor was Dianne Walber. This book was set in Souvenir. It was composed by the McGraw-Hill Book Company Professional & Reference Division composition unit.

Printed and bound by R. R. Donnelley & Sons Company.

CONTENTS

PART SEVEN *Trigger point resources*

INTRODUCTION

Managing the future, beginning now

"Alas, things are not what they used to be."
From the Earliest Writings Ever Discovered

The major theme underlying this book is that the business environment is no longer an extension of the past, but a whole new set of situations we must learn to live with—and master. Some of these situations come from:

- Faster changes in technology, which result in faster obsolescence of previous products and services
- Faster market saturation, because better mass distribution and communication speed up the presentation of products and services to a worldwide market and because expanded consumer and commercial credit facilitate buying power
- Faster competition, because a pioneer's time advantage is shrink-

ing and copycats don't incur the high R&D costs that the innovator must amortize

- Faster segmentation of the market, because we now have a rapidly changing pluralistic society of many different groups rather than the homogeneous mass market of the past
- Faster changes in the external environment create deeper global repercussions. The October 19, 1987, New York stock market crash created a chain reaction throughout the world. It's a vivid, but painful, illustration of the principle of unpredictability. Businesses and their managements are not yet in tune with the speed and magnitude of fluctuations. It takes a new way of looking at the changing world to cope with and to profit from its gyrations.

To have a profitable company today and in the future, "fast" must be an operative word: fast innovation, fast turnarounds, fast technology, fast demographics. An "objective" can still be long-range, but the plans to get there have to change fast and often. It is going to go on being an unpredictable world that throws a lot of curveballs.

Business executives (and politicians) have a harder time than consumers in this new environment. Consumers have a relatively passive role. They have only to adapt to new conditions. Business executives must formulate policy and take actions on changes that no one yet fully understands in all their ramifications. They must be clear in their own minds about their assumptions concerning the future, about the circumstances they can control and the ones they can't, and about the actions they absolutely must take—next Monday morning.

Trigger Points is an action handbook for some of these executives. I say "some" because this isn't a book for managers who charge into action because they've got "this gut feeling" (and little or no information), nor is it for the voracious data gatherers who study the facts to death and end up doing zilch. It's for thinking doers who respect their gut feelings, but check them out—without contracting paralysis from analysis.

PART ONE

Four Trigger Point Assumptions about the World of 1988 to 1993

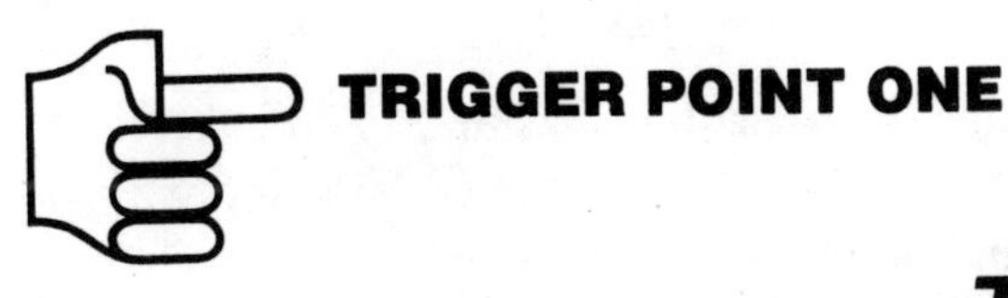

TRIGGER POINT ONE

The only thing we can depend on is unpredictability.

"He who lives by the crystal ball will end up eating ground glass."
Author Unknown

No longer can we look confidently into the future, estimate our costs, take the measure of our competition, and then make a long-range forecast that we can stick to (and even if we are wrong, nothing really bad will happen).

Consider what has happened just in the space of a few years:

- Inflation soared from 3 percent to 18 percent and descended to 3 percent again.
- The prime rate jumped from 6 percent to 22 percent and then fell to 7.5 percent.
- The composite value of the U.S. dollar versus other currencies fell from 100 to 75, then zoomed to 146, and collapsed again versus the Japanese yen, the German mark, and the Swiss franc

(e.g., the dollar fell from 260 yen to 133 yen, the lowest in 40 years).

- Oil went from $3 a barrel to $36, then down to $10 and back up to $18. (Within a few months in 1986, oil fluctuated between $32 and $10.)
- The Iran-Iraq war was predicted to last 6 weeks and to create an oil scarcity; instead, it has been going on for over 6 years and we have the greatest oil glut in history.
- Gold soared from $40 to $800 and experts predicted it would top $1000. It went below $300.
- Silver jumped to $50, and the Hunt brothers lost a huge bundle when it dropped back to $6 and bottomed at $4.
- In 1986, copper was selling at 1932 prices.
- The 1980 promise of a balanced federal budget turned into a $200 billion annual deficit for the next 6 years (and probably more).

Are these just aberrations—exceptions to the norm? No, they indicate a major fundamental change in the world's economic structure. The era of predictability ended in 1973 with the OPEC oil embargo and the first oil shock. Since then we have seen faster and deeper changes in raw material costs, international currencies, stock market prices, trade balances, inflation and interest rates, GNP fluctuations, and world debt structures than ever before in modern industrial and economic history.

Don't Commit Yourself to Something That Probably Won't Happen

Crystal ball gazing is futile in an unpredictable world. Traditionally, CEOs want hard predictions from their managers: "Give me a number." In an era of unpredictability, this doesn't make sense. A forecast is binding; you're committed to it; your reputation is at stake. You can't change your forecast without losing face. So your tendency is to stick to your forecast even if you know it's wrong. That's dangerous.

A Classic Example of the Fallacy of Forecasts: "One of the great miscalculations in IBM history" read the headline of an IBM ad in 1986. The miscalculation was a 1957 forecast that there was a market for only 52 computers in the world. The forecast was based on the estimates of 52 IBM special representatives—experts in specific industries such as banking, insurance, chemicals, and retailing. The forecaster asked these representatives how many of the newfangled computers they would sell. Each said, "One." (Their thinking was that to say "none" would look bad, and to say "two" would be committing themselves to too much.) Thus, 52 computers in the world became the forecast.

Lesson to Be Learned

Don't make forecasts; make *assumptions*. There's a big psychological difference. If things change next month, you can adjust your assumption without losing face.

The One Key Assumption You Must Make

All managers must operate with some basic assumptions to help them set policies and make decisions. The most important assumption you must make now is whether the high swings of the post-1973 era will continue. That is one assumption on which you cannot be flexible, because it determines the way you will run your business. Your choices are:

1. Fluctuations will become greater.
2. Fluctuations will be the same.
3. Fluctuations will be smaller.

Business executives usually feel they must be positive and optimistic about the future, so I have found that the majority choice seems to be that the highs and lows will dampen considerably in the near future.

I disagree. In my opinion, fluctuations will continue at the high rate of the recent past and will be equally unpredictable. Executives should expect the unexpected and be prepared for:

- Rapid changes in consumer demand
- Speedy obsolescence of existing products and markets
- Emergence of new opportunities
- Breakthroughs in technology
- Changes in regulations and deregulations
- Different import-export conditions
- International political impacts on trade and finances
- And much more

Many of these "unpredictables" will be positive; others will create difficulties. Whichever they are, the company must be coolly prepared for the unexpected and have an internal organization that is geared to fast changes and is ready for fast reaction.

These capabilities cannot be wished for. They must be established. The corporate culture must be geared to this unpredictable world by astute leadership of the few executives responsible for the future of the enterprise. Obviously, the first step is an objective analysis of the present.

Why More Knowledge Means More Unpredictability, Not Less

Why has unpredictability become the norm? One major reason is that a basic structural change in our way of living has taken us into a new age: the knowledge age.

All societies evolve with time. The evolution, whether you call it progress or not, is created by the continuously increasing base of human knowledge. Knowledge generates new advances in technology which in turn influence and change our way of life.

Biological evolution is slow and linear; the accumulation of knowledge is exponential and feeds on itself. Therefore, technological breakthroughs also are occurring at an exponential pace. This acceleration presents new opportunities, but also new problems, for the industrialized societies.

A Bit of History: The agricultural society lasted for 5000 years and then was replaced by the industrial society less than 300 years ago. In the United States, the industrial economy was superseded by the service economy in 1956, the year in which, for the first time, there were more service workers than industrial workers. By 1986, 75 percent of the U.S. work force was in the service sector—and only 18 percent in manufacturing.

Quite suddenly, during the late 1970s, the age of information and knowledge was born. It was made possible by the explosion of electronics and computer and communications technology. It can now be said that the major currency in this new world economy is knowledge, replacing the old currencies of grain (Egyptians), salt (the Middle Ages), spices (Renaissance), gold, and oil.

The underlying concept throughout this book is that the new knowledge era is not an extension of the past; it represents a structural change fundamentally different from the known and familiar. That is why it is not yet completely understood in all its aspects and ramifications. Some executives would argue that our increased access to knowledge should serve to reduce unpredictability—I believe just the opposite. In fact, I have not so modestly called this the *Kami paradox:*

The increased rate of knowledge creates increased unpredictability.

Why is this? First, increased knowledge speeds the rate of technological breakthroughs—which in turn speed the rate at which products become obsolete. When I was IBM's Director of Product Planning in the 1950s, the cycle of obsolescence for IBM products was 9 years. Now it is under 3 years. This, of course, makes it more difficult to recoup one's investment in new products. Each golden goose has a shorter life.

The increased rate of knowledge has created better educated, more sophisticated consumers—another reason for increased unpredictability. Because the U.S. economy depends on consumers, their feelings, desires, and fears become crucially important and basically determine the direction of the economy. Today, they are more demanding and individualistic—and less and less predictable.

Energy Use No Longer Determines Our Standard of Living

What's happened to our consumption of energy strikingly illustrates the new era of knowledge and unpredictability. For over 150 years of industrial progress, energy consumption was directly proportional to GNP growth. In fact, economists won a Nobel prize in 1970 for concepts including the formula that the standard of living in a country is directly proportional to the amount of energy consumed per capita.

However, since 1973—the year of the oil embargo—the real GNP increased 45 percent and the consumption of energy *went down 36 percent.* Obviously, something no longer computes. And this reversal of the relation between the use of energy and the standard of living has occurred in all of the industrialized countries of the world—and most countries in the Third World as well.

This development was due to technological breakthroughs made possible by the new knowledge era. By raising the price of energy to impossible levels, OPEC forced industrial countries into higher and higher technologies and radically different ways of doing things: microminiaturization, computers, communications, conservation, achievement of the same results with less weight and material. This is one reason why "smokestack America" is now called the Rust Belt.

Why Bother Planning in an Unpredictable World?

Changes are occurring faster, and the future becomes more unpredictable. So why plan ahead? Is realistic planning even possible? The answer is an emphatic yes to both. In fact, planning is far more essential under conditions of unpredictability than in a stable environment.

Planning today requires more innovation and a continuous, detailed input of external trends and factors. "Suppose if" scenarios are essential, and so is an ongoing examination and testing of the organization's ability to respond to unpredictable events. An organization must be capable of reversing a past decision or action without catastrophic effects.

The key word on top of our thinking pyramid must be *flexibility*. Flexibility should be built into every major action taken by a company; otherwise, the company will not be able to respond to new developments and breakthroughs.

A Case of Nonflexibility. After billions of dollars were spent on the Alaskan pipeline, the crude oil cannot be taken to nearby California refineries. Instead, huge supertankers must take the oil the long way through the Gulf of Mexico to Texas refineries. The reason: California refineries were not designed to handle oil with high sulfur content. Flexibility had not been built into the plants.

A Case of Flexibility. In the great diaper war between Procter & Gamble and Kimberly-Clark, P&G got to the market first with new diapers that incorporated a chemical so superabsorbent that far less cellulose fluff was needed. As a result, P&G's market share climbed from 47 to 56 percent in 1986, while Kimberly-Clark's dropped to 28 percent. How did P&G get the jump on its major competitor? The New York Times reports: "When P&G invested $500 million to retool its diaper machines in 1985 to compete more effectively with Kimberly-Clark's form-fitting diapers, it had the foresight to make the machines flexible enough so they could later be adjusted to churn out the thinner, superabsorbent diapers without major delay or investment."

Flexibility does not come cheap. As a rough formula, it costs 40 percent more than nonflexibility—in up-front money. But in an unpredictable world, the alternative to buying flexibility can be business failure.

There are many ways to adapt to unpredictability. That's what this book is all about. Adapting to unpredictability is not only possible but is also exciting and highly profitable for the winners—while the inflexible defenders of the past fall by the wayside. The difference between winning and losing lies in the kind of leadership and management philosophy at the top.

TRIGGER POINT TWO

Our economic output is slowing down—and our standard of living isn't rising as fast as it used to.

"There is nothing permanent except change."
HERACLITUS (501 BC)

One of the most important things for a manager to understand about our new economic world can be summed up in a few words: We have a zero-sum economy, so the choice is kill or be killed.

What is a zero-sum economy? Basically, it is one that is not growing in terms of population and standard of living. Thus, according to Thurow's zero-sum principle, for every segment of the economy that grows 10 or 20 percent, another segment must shrink at a corresponding rate.

During the high-growth 1960s, business strategies were based on "more, more, more." It was the era of addition. During the 1980s and beyond, strategies must be based on "instead, instead, instead."

Case in Point 1: In 1980, 42 million suits were made in the U.S.—26 million men's suits and 16 million women's suits. In 1986, the output of suits was only slightly higher than in 1980. The startling change was that we made 10 million more *women's* suits than *men's* suits (because of the sharp jump in the number of working women).

Case in Point 2: Sales of soft drinks are growing faster than the population. With a nearly flat population growth, another beverage has to be a loser—because people can drink only so much liquid.

In this case, coffee is the loser. This is an example of the zero-sum principle in action.

Lesson to Be Learned

It's the era of *replacement* and *substitution*. The consumer will not buy a house *and* a car *and* a boat *and* college educations for the children. It will be *either* this *or* that *or* something else. It becomes imperative to understand the changing markets and customers' priorities and the changing moods and mores of our complex society. The easy shotgun approach must give way to tough rifle precision.

The zero-sum principle applies to individual companies as well as to the economy as a whole. For every company that grows at 15 percent a year, there must be one that fails at the same rate. In the "good old days," excellent, good, and mediocre companies could coexist. Today, there's no such thing as coexistence—poor performers must decay and go out of business.

What we have today is absolute market maturity—not just for some products but for all products. The reason: Population growth has all but stopped. In 1987, the U.S. population growth is a low 0.9 percent. That breaks down to 0.7 percent children and 0.2 percent immigrants (who generally don't have much money to spend). And we can't expect population growth to go up, because of a very simple fact: The number of children born is inversely proportional to the amount of education people have. As families become more affluent and educated, the birthrate plunges.

The industrial world's population will grow at less than 0.5 percent per year, an almost fourfold decrease from the past. Political changes will not reverse this trend, because they have little influence on childbearing rates. The slowdown of the world's economic growth is apolitical.

Fact: We Have a Basically Flat Standard of Living

The decrease in population growth is accompanied by another basic structural change in our economy: a corresponding decrease in the growth of the U.S. standard of living.

Why is this so important to our economy? Because our economy is based on consumers. Personal income of Americans represents 83 percent of GNP. *Disposable* personal income represents 70 percent of GNP.

The consumer makes or breaks the economy, because the health of the country is directly related to the rate of increase of real per capita consumer income and spending. All other factors are minor: Capital investment depends on consumer demand; exports are offset by imports; and national defense spending ends up mostly in consumers' pockets.

I've developed a quarterly index that tells it all. It represents per capita consumer spending in constant dollars—modified to exclude expenditures that do not directly contribute to a better individual standard of living (taxes, excessively high utility rates and casualty insurance premiums, above-average medical costs).

The Kami Index shows that the true standard of living has gone up only 8 points in 15 years—an extremely slow increase. An even more startling figure is that, since about 1970, the median income of families in constant dollars has been absolutely flat.

This leads to a significant conclusion: People have the same amount of money, but they are spending it differently. The standard of living has not increased—it has *changed.*

The Battle for Customers Grows Fiercer

Our zero-sum economy represents a basic structural change that requires new business strategies. We are a consumer-oriented economy—but we're not getting our traditional supply of new consumers, and their disposable income is not increasing.

The result is that we are entering an era of fierce competition. What some call a temporary period of slow growth and stagnation is in reality the new "normal" state. With fewer potential new customers, the battle is on to grab them—often at any cost. This battle is further complicated by fast technological obsolescence and the greater volatility of consumer moods and tastes.

All this doesn't mean there aren't tremendous opportunities for business growth. The opportunities are there, but they exist within a brand new framework and they cannot be exploited by traditional business strategies. Unless you understand the dynamic changes that are taking place, you will be in the wrong market at the wrong time—and thinking in the wrong way.

TRIGGER POINT THREE

We'll have a high rate of chronic unemployment for some time to come.

"Every day cannot be a feast of lanterns."
Chinese Proverb

It's not a pleasant thought, but an important basic change in U.S. society is the presence of pervasive, chronic unemployment. That's true even when there's an economic boom. During the 14 years from 1973 to 1987, real GNP increased 38 percent, the population grew 24 percent, and the labor force rose 38 percent—but unemployment soared *90* percent. "There's no longer a direct link between prosperity in the marketplace and jobs," according to Harley Shaiken, a labor professor at the University of California at San Diego.

There's a logical explanation for this phenomenon (though it is of little solace to the 7 million plus unemployed). The labor participation rate—that is, the percentage of the U.S. adult population in the labor force—was stabilized for decades at around 56 percent. It started climbing in 1973, and it reached 61 percent in 1987.

This 5-point differential seems small, but it represents 9.2 million additional and "unexpected" entrants into the labor pool. They are mostly women because of changes in our social structure: need for two incomes, women's liberation movement, single parents, and higher divorce rate.

At the same time, the *need* for additional labor has *declined*. Reasons:

- Increased foreign competition from imports—made possible by higher productivity, lower labor costs, and technological progress in Japan, South Korea, and other countries
- Automation and productivity gains in the United States—leading, for example, to a labor force reduction of 30 percent in the automobile industry
- Change in types of industry—such as the trend toward miniaturization, which has reduced the need for labor-intensive production

Another major factor behind the higher unemployment rate is what's happening to the ranks of middle management: They're being decimated. For years, headquarters staffs were expanding into huge, multilayer "corpocracies." Now downsizing has taken over. Thousands of white-collar workers who assumed their jobs were for life are finding themselves out on the street.

Exxon reduced its headquarters staff from 2300 to 325 in just a little more than 10 years. In 1987, General Motors announced plans to lose 25,000 middle managers. By then, Ford had already cut its salaried work force by 30 percent and planned to eliminate another 20 percent. Those are just a few examples of what's taking place all over corporate America.

The downsizing trend isn't just temporary; it's long-term. Relentless foreign competition has forced most U.S. corporations to make "operating mean and lean" a way of life. Computers have made many middle-management jobs redundant. So has the ceaseless flood of mergers, acquisitions, and corporate reorganizations.

What Happened to the "Indispensable" Middle Manager?

The change in attitude toward white-collar workers reflects the change in the competitive position of American corporations in the world market. With Japanese and European industry lying in ruins at the end of World War II, American companies had the world market to themselves. Both at home and abroad, the main challenge was supplying demand. With success so easy, the leaders of many large companies worried mostly about preventing failure. So they began to assemble giant corporate staffs made up of business-school graduates to keep an eye on operations.

But the bureaucracy grew so large at the Chrysler Corporation that middle managers were mindlessly turning out reports whose original purpose had long been forgotten. At Xerox, operating divisions had to obtain corporate approval of such minor decisions as the color scheme of copiers or increasing the intensity of a light bulb in a given machine. And General Electric made some key blunders in the 1970s—such as designing a line of smaller refrigerators—because hordes of key strategic planners who were out of touch with the marketplace were calling the shots.

The rise in the late 1970s and early 1980s of truly formidable foreign competition, coupled with deregulation and recession, made high management costs too heavy a burden. "Older companies are now reorganizing themselves very quickly under the force of competition," said Audrey Freedman, a labor economist at the Conference Board, a business-research organization in New York City.

From an article by Steven Prokesch in The New York Times, *March 22, 1987.*

Our New Full-Employment Standard: 7 Percent Out of Work

The help-wanted index in *The Wall Street Journal* is a good indication of the lessening demand for personnel. In recent good years it ranged from 130 to 140—well below the previous high of 165. That is not a fluke; it is another basic structural change. The full-employment standard for the United States has been practically (if not politically) changed from the traditional 4 percent to 7 percent.

This change is significant for consumer-oriented companies, because it has created a larger low-income market segment. We now have a bimodal distribution of U.S. consumers: low earners and unemployed at one end, high earners at the other—and a void in the middle. The low-income market is big: 36 percent of all households earn less than $15,000. Research by economics professors Barry Bluestone and Bennett Harrison shows that, between 1979 and 1985, almost half—44 percent—of the net new jobs created in the United States paid poverty-level wages. That is more than twice the rate of low-wage job creation that prevailed during the 1960s and 1970s.

This situation calls for new marketing strategies by companies that want to stay profitable—strategies we will discuss in detail later.

TRIGGER POINT FOUR

The mass market is splitting apart and, more than ever, the customer is the ultimate ruler.

"Small opportunities are often the beginning of great enterprises."
DEMOSTHENES (352 BC)

Just a few years ago, Coca-Cola sold two cola drinks: Coke and Tab. Today the company markets new Coke, Coca-Cola Classic, caffeine-free Coke, diet Coke, caffeine-free diet Coke, cherry Coke, diet cherry Coke, and Tab with and without calcium, and these products come in cans, glass bottles, and plastic bottles for a total of at least 42 different permutations.

This is just one example of a major structural change in our economy: the end of mass production. Henry Ford's successful formula that "You can have any color car you want as long as it's black" is deader than a doornail. We no longer have the biggest homogeneous mass market in the world. Instead, consumers are segmented, polarized, and more individualistic.

Understanding this phenomenon is absolutely essential to any company that wants to survive and prosper. It means that, more than ever, customers are the ultimate rulers.

A platitude? Of course, but also a basic truth. And to satisfy these ultimate rulers, businesses must learn to produce many varieties, product extensions, flavors, colors, models, and types through short but profitable runs.

Another basic truth: The U.S. economy depends on the consumers. He and she represent officially about 64 percent of the total GNP—but in reality it is 99 percent because the 15 percent business investment sector builds, expands, and innovates for the consumer. The 20 percent government segment also supports the consumer economy. Although consumers don't buy tanks and missiles, many consumers work for defense subcontractors and spend their money on goods and services.

The End Customer Is Emperor

Many companies boast of their customer orientation but are concerned only with the direct buyers of their products or services. They should also understand and respect their customers' customers' customers' customers: the ultimate users. If the customer is king, the ultimate user is emperor. This is true whether the business is mining, retailing, machining, banking, construction, or nuclear power production.

The ultimate customer can be lovable, unsophisticated, sincere, irrational. Regardless, he or she wields absolute power over the destiny of any business.

Case in Point 1: A manufacturer of custom gears may sell its products to packaging machinery fabricators who make complex, high-speed assembly lines for filling, sealing, and labeling tin and aluminum cans. Their customers are soup makers like Heinz and Campbell, who in turn market to the ultimate user, Mr. and Ms. America. When Mr. and Ms. America decide that they prefer dry soup mixes or the new plastic Tetra Brik container, Heinz and Campbell will not wait long to replace cans by using a different packaging method. The canning machinery market will shrink, and the gears supplier will be out of business without even knowing what hit it.

Case in Point 2: A producer of butadiene, a petrochemical derivative, sells the compound to a synthetic rubber manufacturer, who supplies tire makers, who sell to automobile factories, who sell transportation to the ultimate consumer. When that consumer decides to buy small cars, which use smaller tires, the butadiene maker is left sitting on a huge stockpile of unwanted chemicals.

Understanding the New Consumer

Who is the ultimate consumer we're talking about? That's important to know in today's pluralistic, segmented, individualistic society. Yet psychological economics—the understanding of the feelings and behavior patterns of the consumer—is too often neglected, especially when the ultimate consumer is many levels away.

We can identify some major shifts that the ultimate consumer has undergone in recent years:

- *Smaller families.* The no-children family has grown 34 percent since 1970; the one-to-two-children family has grown 18 percent; and the three-or-more-children family has *shrunk* 44 percent. Smaller households affect product design, e.g., the need for compact appliances and one-portion prepared foods. This, in turn, requires massive changes in parts manufacturing and packaging machinery.
- *Desire for more leisure.* Formerly, the work ethic had priority.
- *Better education.* The consequences are higher discrimination and awareness of value.
- *Polarization.* The middle class is eroding, and companies must aim high or low.
- *Segmentation.* Consumers are no longer a homogeneous mass market.
- *More skepticism.* Consumers are not as trusting as they used to be; they cannot be fooled as easily. Companies must make their

advertising more real. (Look at Holiday Inn, which mounted a major ad campaign based on "No Surprises" and ended up getting twice as many customer complaints as normal because it couldn't live up to that promise.)

- *More individualism.* Companies cannot assume that all consumers think alike.
- *Greater power for female consumers.* Working women, professional women, and single heads of households have more independence, individuality, and strength. The traditional U.S. family—working father, homemaker wife, and two or more kids—represents only 7 percent of today's approximately 85 million households. More than 54 percent of mothers work, and one-quarter of all households are run by single parents.
- *More older consumers.* Our population is aging, and older consumers have different needs and values than younger ones. The target is no longer the 18-to-34 group; it is the 25-to-45 group. This is a smarter, more skeptical, better-educated group. It wants value, and it is less swayed by hucksterism.
- *More impatience.* Consumers are increasingly intolerant of bad service, such as slow deliveries.
- *More insistence.* Merchants and manufacturers will have to honor their commitments.
- *Less formality.* The trend is toward the casual in apparel, dining, travel, and accessories.
- *Less brand loyalty.* National brands will have to provide additional real value and prove their uniqueness or differentiation.

It is important for executives to understand all of these changes and to identify with them. The next step is to analyze the direct and indirect effect of these and other factors on the purchasing habits and needs of the consumer. The analysis should then be evaluated from the producer's perspective to provide advance information on the future demand for the line of products and services of one's company.

What Happened to the Middle Class?

Most U.S. businesses traditionally have aimed their marketing at the famous "middle class." We've all seen the familiar curve: a minority of poor at one end, rich at the other, and everyone else massed under a big hump in the middle.

That hump no longer exists. The middle of the curve is sinking lower and lower; it is being replaced by twin humps—the lower middle class and the upper middle class.

The traditional middle class—defined as families with annual incomes of $15,000 to $35,000—fell from 51 percent of the total in 1973 to 39 percent in 1985. The top 20 percent of American families (those earning over $48,000) received 43 percent of all income in 1985—a post–World War II high. The bottom 20 percent (those earning under $13,200) got 4.7 percent of all income—the lowest in 25 years.

What happened to the middle class? It lost its basic underpinnings: the blue-collar, industrial, high-union-wage sector. This sector is being eroded by manufacturing downsizing, foreign competition, reduced union power, and automation.

Today's—and tomorrow's—growth is in the services and trades sectors; they create 9 out of 10 new jobs. Since 1980, approximately 23 million jobs have shifted from manufacturing to service. While a good manufacturing union worker in Detroit will make $25,000 to $30,000 a year, a supermarket checker will make $9000 to $11,000. This shift has created an enormous lower middle class.

The upper middle class consists primarily of three groups:

- Working couples—joint earners each of whom makes $15,000 to $20,000 create annual family incomes of $30,000 to $40,000.
- Technicians—such as programmers, who can make $40,000 to $50,000 annually.
- Supervisors—more of them in service businesses, making $40,000 a year.

Don't Shoot for the Middle!

We're talking about a crucially important structural change. Half of the new jobs come from four industries: health, business services, finance, and eating/drinking places. By 1990, the latter will add 3 times the number of jobs existing in the entire computer industry. More than half of the 8 million new U.S. jobs created from 1979 to 1984 paid under $7000 a year, while the middle-income share of job growth dropped from 64.2 percent in the 1970s to 47.5 percent in the early 1980s.

These are dry statistics, but they are overwhelmingly significant. The poorer are getting poorer; the rich are getting richer; and the middle is shrinking. We are developing into a polarized society. This has tremendous implications for businesses in terms of strategies, production, development, and marketing.

The basic lesson is: "Don't aim for the middle!" Not all companies seem to recognize this.

Case in Point: Sears is a retailing giant that employs a phalanx of economists. But its marketing strategy suggests that it is not paying attention to what is happening to U.S. society today. The median income of U.S. families is about $27,000; the median income of Sears' customers is $27,850. Sears is aiming at precisely the wrong spot—smack in the middle. That's why Sears is losing market share to downscale stores such as Wal-Mart and upscale stores such as Bloomingdale's.

How to Succeed in a Polarized Society

The polarization of consumers calls for a corresponding strategy: the deliberate polarization of one's products and services. The customer wants either natural fibers or synthetic blends, hand-crafted rosewood cabinets or mass-produced laminate-covered particleboard cabinets.

Products, services, retail outlets, merchandising, advertising, quality/value, manufacturing, management style, and policies must all be geared to the new two-culture society. Make your choice and adapt. If you want to serve all three masters—the growing low, shrinking middle, and growing high—organize for each one separately. Don't have Mercedes and VW in the same showroom.

The focus must be sharp: a Hyundai for the lower middle class, a Corvette for the upper middle class. A car aimed squarely at the middle will be a loser.

So-So Will Be No-Go

Polarized business strategy avoids so-so, middle-of the road products and services. Instead, it aims at:

- Excellent service or no service
- Expensive goods or cheap goods
- High quality or minimal quality (disposables)
- Luxury or basic utility
- First class or no-frills superthrift
- Dom Perignon or André champagne

Pluralism Replaces the Mass Market

To polarization must be added a second momentous change in the makeup of U.S. consumers: They are becoming pluralistic and segmented. It's no longer a monolithic market out there—and only a business that understands this can succeed.

Polarization is based on income, while segmentation is based on many other factors such as age, race, religion, location, tastes, and ethnicity. These are just some of the cells of segmentation. You may have hundreds of them—and for each one you need a specific penetration strategy. You can no longer say, "Let's put out four different models of Product X and see who's going to buy them."

Nor do you use the same marketing approach for 19-year-olds that you do for 65-year-olds.

Getting to Know You: A Look at Our Segmented Consumer Society

How do you learn more about the many different segments of our consumer society? From many sources—we'll talk about the useful technique of razor blade reading later in the book. But one particularly comprehensive source of information that can help in developing segmented strategies is psychographics—the study of different values and lifestyles (VALS) in the United States. The Stanford Research Institute has conducted extensive research on this subject. SRI has identified four major groups of people and nine VALS types within those groups. Here's a brief summary:

1. OUTER-DIRECTED (108 million people or 67 percent of the adult population)
   a. *Belongers (57 million, 36 percent)*
      - Aging
      - Traditional
      - Conventional
      - Contented
      - Intensely patriotic
      - Moral
      - Family-oriented
      - Conforming
      - Nonexperimental
      - Sentimental
      - Deeply stable
      - Want to fit in, not stand out
   b. *Achievers (35 Million, 22 Percent)*
      - Middle-aged
      - Prosperous
      - Gifted
      - Hardworking
      - Successful
      - Able leaders

- Self-assured
- Materialistic
- Builders of the American Dream
- Staunchly conservative
- Opposed to any radical changes

c. *Emulators (16 Million, 10 Percent)*
- Youthful
- Striving
- Ambitious
- Macho
- Show-off
- Competitive
- Very hardworking
- Fairly successful
- Trying to break into the system
- Trying to make it big

2. INNER-DIRECTED (32 million, 20 percent)

a. *Societally Conscious (13 Million, 8 Percent)*
- Mission-oriented
- Concerned
- Leaders of single-issue groups
- Mature
- Successful
- Influential
- Nature-oriented
- Less materialistic, sometimes live in voluntary simplicity

b. *Experientials (11 Million, 7 Percent)*
- Youthful
- Well-educated
- Have well-paid technical and professional jobs
- Seek direct experience
- Deeply involved
- Person-centered
- Artistic
- Intensely oriented toward inner growth
- Experimental
- Politically liberal
- No faith in institutions

c. *I-Am-Me (8 Million, 5 Percent)*

- Young (average age 21)
- Transition stage
- Confused
- Can be both exhibitionistic and demure
- Can be both narcissistic and self-effacing
- Impulsive
- Dramatic
- Experimental
- Active
- Very innovative

3. NEED-DRIVEN (17 million, 11 percent)
   a. *Sustainers (11 million, 7 percent)*
      - Living on edge of poverty
      - Angry, distrustful, resentful
      - Rebellious, combative
      - Streetwise
      - Involved in underground economy
      - Still hopeful
   b. *Survivors (6 Million, 4 Percent)*
      - Old
      - Intensely poor
      - Fearful
      - Depressed
      - Despairing
      - Far removed from the cultural mainstream
      - Misfits
      - Poorly educated
      - Ill
      - Conservative
      - Unhappy about fast change
      - Lost hope
4. OUTER/INNER-DIRECTED (3 million, 2 percent)
   a. *Integrated (3 Million, 2 Percent)*
      - Psychologically mature
      - Large field of vision—global perspective
      - Tolerant and understanding
      - Sense of fittingness
      - Makers and movers
      - Observers and creators

- Open
- Self-assured
- Self-expressive

Each of these categories is large enough to justify the development of products and services specifically designed to fit the socioeconomic and psychological characteristics of the people within the group. Of course, these categories may be further defined, refined, and segmented for precise target marketing. That calls for a greater investment in detailed demographic and psychographic data.

Stanford Research Institute, Daniel Yankelovich, and others have different ways of classifying the pluralistic consumer. It's important to know their approaches and choose the one that's most appropriate for one's business.

Even the Census Bureau has provided an interesting consumer category: persons of the opposite sex sharing living quarters (POSSLQ). The census people created this category for the 1980 census because the family classification implied a marital relationship.

POSSLQs can stimulate the following derivative thinking: apartment renters rather than house dwellers (less permanency); small and inexpensive furniture (young, with little money); furniture rental rather than purchase. The furniture rental market grew some 600 percent between 1975 and 1985.

Betting on the Baby-Boomers

Baby-boomers represent an extremely important and different segment of the U.S. consumer market. There are 77 million of them—born between 1946 and 1964—comprising one-third of the U.S. population. They will account for 50 percent of all consumer expenditures by 1990, so it pays to get to know their needs and tastes.

What are they like? They're sophisticated, affluent, educated. Raised on television, they have a mix of traditional values and liberal traits. They bear fewer children, marry more, and divorce more, and a third of them are yuppies (young urban professionals). Over 69 percent of female baby-boomers work for pay.

Know your baby-boomers—it's vital to marketing success. Here's a rundown of their lifestyles and buying preferences:

Cars:

- Foreign styling
- Convertibles
- Sporty look
- Personal transportation

Clothing:

- Casual (but not denim)
- Neat

Fitness:

- Physical exercise
- Tennis
- Skiing
- Racquetball
- Gym
- Sauna
- Jogging
- Resorts with action
- Active travel

Cuisine:

- Sophisticated
- Experimental
- Varied menu
- Ethnic

- Fresh foods
- Healthful
- Convenience in preparation, packaging, and portions

Housing:

- Smaller but chic
- More amenities, appliances, and gadgets
- More outdoor areas for leisure time
- Better-quality furniture
- Esthetically superior

Work Environment:

- Demand for more benefits such as insurance, free time, and pleasant surroundings
- Less loyalty
- Less mobility (working couples)

Technology Use:

- Computers
- Telephones and other communicating devices
- Time-saving devices
- Fastest form of travel

Our Economy Depends on Consumer Whims—So You'd Better Know What They Are

The nonessentials in life are actually very essential to the U.S. economy. Although it has stopped growing, the already high U.S.

standard of living permits an average family to spend 40 percent of its income on items that are beyond the necessities of subsistence. That is a huge slice of the economy; in fact, 25 percent of the entire GNP is at the mercy of the fickle likes and dislikes of the consumer.

Considering that a 5 percent growth of the real GNP is a boom and a 5 percent decline is a bust, the discretionary whims of the consumer must be well understood, because they control the economy. That's why it's so important to spot trends early and identify new markets before your competition does. Shotgun marketing is out; marketing must now have the pinpoint precision of a rifle.

Polarization and segmentation mean that specialties and niche products will thrive. In later chapters, we will discuss Monday morning actions you can take to exploit the tremendous opportunities presented by today's individualistic consumers.

PART TWO

Choosing Your Basic Strategy for Success in an Unpredictable World

TRIGGER POINT FIVE

An outside-in strategy is the only sensible option.

"The downfall of a magician is belief in his own magic."

Author Unknown

Many companies are in deep trouble for one reason: They plan from the inside out instead of the outside in. Inside-out companies focus inwardly. They let their corporate capabilities, strengths, geographical locations, and executive whims determine their policies and actions. In this time of world competition and rapid technological and social change, such an inside-out approach is suicidal—even for giants who once prided themselves on making or controlling the market. Procter & Gamble found that out; General Motors is—or should be—finding that out.

Powerful clichés and images of the past are simply no longer valid today. Companies don't mold the public; they don't create a market; they don't change society. Instead, consumers and external forces create demands for new products, new services, new ways in which the public wants to be served.

There's nothing remarkable about this statement. But many

companies with a long history of success have failed recently because they refused to accept this new fact of life. Corporate graveyards are littered with businesses that did not adapt because they could not see the obvious: Braniff, AM International, Lionel, Continental Illinois, Storage Technologies, Food Fair, International Harvester, Atari, Wickes—and many more previously prosperous companies that either disappeared or became very sick.

Because of their inside-out strategies, U.S. corporate giants missed the boat on:

- The small car
- Overnight package deliveries
- The personal computer
- The working woman
- Ethnic foods
- Subculture market segmentation
- New life insurance policies
- The blue-collar evolution
- Health and diet emphasis
- Craving for convenience
- Demographic migration
- Changed reading habits

And that's just a sampling.

The Four Deadly Sins of Inside-Out Thinking

It takes successful companies many years to accumulate their enviable records of growth and profitability—but just one major strategic mistake can plunge an enterprise into the red. In today's era of extremes, these yearly losses can run to hundreds of millions of dollars (U.S. Steel, British Airways, International Harvester, Pan

Am, Crocker National Bank, Coleco). The turnaround and recovery are painful and difficult; examples are not hard to find:

- Airlines misread the growth of air travel and expanded beyond market capacity. They further compounded their errors by engaging in fare wars.
- Steel companies neglected modernization and capital investment—and lost out to foreign competition.
- Banks increased their risk by plunging into foreign exchange speculation and foreign loans.
- Carmakers underestimated the competition and ignored changing customer desires.
- Smaller computer companies came out of their specialized niches and tried to attack the giants head-on. They lost.
- Door-to-door merchandisers rang door bells and found nobody home. They ignored the fact that a majority of women are in the work force.

What led to these corporate errors? Basically, the answer can be summed up in the four deadly sins of inside-out thinking:

1. *Complacency.* Typified by A&P, a company with a major market share, a historical reputation—and a senile, don't-rock-the-boat management.
2. *Blindness.* Failure to recognize major technological changes (AM International didn't see the shift from electromechanical to electronic technology) or major market changes (Lionel overlooked the switch from trains to games).
3. *Megalomania.* One-man-show management by a benevolent or not so benevolent dictator who relies on intuition ("don't confuse me with the facts"). Example: Lawrence of Braniff with rainbow-colored planes, a billion-dollar international expansion—and rotten service caused by rotten morale.
4. *Greed.* Obsession with short-term, fast-buck superprofits to the detriment of the future. Example: Continential Illinois' ex-

cessively risky loans to the oil industry and Third World countries.

Oops!—or Excellence Revisited

Remember *In Search of Excellence*? Published in 1982, it became the all-time business best-seller in the United States. Authors Thomas J. Peters and Robert H. Waterman, Jr. studied the managements of supergrowth companies with long track records of great performances.

From their research, the authors derived a persuasive cookbook recipe of eight key attributes of excellence. Many companies started applying those guidelines verbatim. They reorganized their operations and changed their "cultures" in pursuit of instant success.

Two years later, serious doubts were being raised about the validity of the book's conclusions. It is now evident that almost half of the 43 companies selected for the "excellence" class no longer deserve (and some never deserved) that classification.

What went wrong with those companies? What is wrong with the now-famous recommendations of Peters and Waterman? Why the fall from excellence? Here are some answers:

- *Texas Instruments.* Lacked understanding of consumer markets, watches, and home computers—and lost $660 million. TI was once a superbly managed company. Its mistake was to say: "Our technological superiority will bring business." Wrong. Technological superiority will bring business—but only if you also have technological *exclusivity*. In today's environment you don't have that very long, so you need marketing, marketing, marketing and quality, quality, quality *in addition* to technological superiority. Unfortunately, TI's engineer-directed marketing strategy emphasized technology rather than customer needs. The company's complex management system was based on an unwieldy matrix concept and number-crunching planning. It was a false decentralization ruled by czars.

- *Xerox.* Tried to compete head-on in the tough computer field—and that turned out to be an expensive ego trip. Management took its eye off its golden goose copier business, lost position everywhere, and did not learn from past errors. As a result, it's down to 20 percent of the copier market. Moreover, Xerox's billion-dollar buy of an insurance and financial services business will haunt the company in the same way as did the disastrous SDS acquisition (computers to compete with IBM) of the 1960s.

- *Walt Disney Productions.* Was wedded too long to a pervasive, unchanging culture. It failed to understand and respond to the changing tastes of the movie and amusement park customer. Disney management was family-oriented, ignoring the reality that this was no longer true of their customers. Out of 13 Disney films, only *Splash* was a success—and it happened to be the one film that was produced without going through the Disney review board. Now Disney's new management is making successful R-rated films such as *Down and Out in Beverly Hills.*

- *Atari.* Victim of video game superboom and superbust, out-of-control management, and lack of market understanding. Atari's errors cost $500 million, and the company dwindled from 7000 employees to a few hundred in 7 years.

- *Caterpillar Tractor.* After 48 years of profitable operations, Caterpillar made the mistake of believing its own forecast. In 1975, Cat's thinking was: "The world's infrastructure is crumbling, so it will need more roads, more bridges, more dams, more construction." Caterpillar then proceeded to invest $2 billion in new capacity. Logically, that was correct. But the world said, "Let the infrastructure crumble, we don't have the money." The heavy-machinery market dropped by 30 percent. *Lesson to be learned:* Don't make forecasts, and if you do, don't stick to them. Instead, move with the flow.

  Second Catepillar mistake: arrogance. Senior managers said that their Japanese competition, Komatsu, would never achieve their distribution, their service, their quality. Like Detroit automakers, Caterpillar found out differently.

Now Caterpillar is getting back into the black. Why? Because much of its equipment is now made in South Korea. It announced the closing of nine U.S. plants and as of 1987, laid off 40 percent of its work force

- *Fluor.* Made a disastrous acquisition of St. Joe Minerals for $2.3 billion in 1981—just before metal prices collapsed. The strategic purpose was to offset fluctuating construction contracts with a solid-base market. But Fluor picked the wrong market, and its stock dropped from 71 to 15.
- *Levi Strauss.* Arrogance, arrogance, arrogance. With 80 percent of the jeans market, its reps told the buyer: "You're going to buy so many dozen of this color and that style; I'll write it for you; you sign it; and you better behave or else." The buyer signed, but inside was thinking: "One of these days I'll show that SOB." That opportunity eventually came because Strauss was manufacturing-oriented rather than marketing-oriented. It lost out on the shift to fashion jeans, innovative merchandising, and advertising. It made the wrong acquisitions and was slow to respond to change. Now it's laying off people, decentralizing, reducing staff, and fighting to regain markets and vitality.

Most of these companies will rebound and be profitable once more. But why didn't the Peters-Waterman formula continue to work for them?

The answer is surprisingly simple. The flaw of the famous eight attributes for excellence is that they are a set of rigid formulas. Formulas don't work any more. They must be replaced by flexibility, outside-in strategy, and adaptation to change. Look at the diverse ways in which success has been achieved:

- Iacocca saved Chrysler through centralization and one-man rule; IBM captured the personal computer market by decentralizing the PC division and making it almost autonomous.
- Dow Jones succeeds by sticking to its knitting; 3M succeeds by producing a multiplicity of unrelated products.
- Miller pioneered its way to temporary success; Anheuser-Busch won the war by being "second with power."

- Lincoln Electric achieves productivity through people; Seiko and Canon achieve it through automation.
- K-Mart succeeds by discounting goods and providing minimal service; Neiman-Marcus does well by featuring premium price and personal attention.

Each company must adapt to its own situation in its own way. The common denominator is the ability to sense a change in the external environment early on and deliver a fast, innovative response.

You Must Be Alert to Outside Changes

External events shape the future of any organization. That's why the organization must have a responsive, adaptive, innovative internal environment geared to detecting external changes and reacting to them quickly. Outside-in management means *clue analysis.* (Of which, more later.) Every member of the team must be a detective of change, an architect of change, an agent of change.

Managers must understand and evaluate the changing nature of the 10 E's:

- *Economics*—high real interest rates, world interdependence, deficits, deeper fluctuations
- *Energy*—price uncertainty, changing demand
- *Ecology*—higher operating costs, social responsibility
- *Establishment*—governmental regulation/deregulation, taxes
- *Ethics*—white-collar crime, executive and business behavior
- *Evolution*—rate of adaptation to social and technological change
- *Expectations*—changes in consumer, customer, and public demand for goods, services, and performance

- *Entitlement*—employees' needs and requests for pay, benefits, rewards, incentives, and work environment
- *Employment*—changing skill needs, automation, layoffs, and productivity
- *Education*—training at all levels, increasing sophistication, and talent shortage

Every business unit must evaluate the impact of such external changes on its operations and performance.

How to Be an Outside-In Company

The tools are known. They include:

- Good market research, continuous scanning and marketplace analysis, and real understanding of the ultimate user's needs and wishes.
- An unbiased management audit, continuous evaluation of the company's ability to react to ultimate user demand and to changes in socioeconomic conditions in the United States and abroad.
- A strong talent pool: One cannot succeed with dummies.

All of these will be discussed later on in terms of next Monday morning actions. But it should be pointed out now that these tools must be supported by something else that is urgently needed by every organization: a healthy dose of plain common sense.

The outside-in company is neither pessimistic nor optimistic; instead, it is realistic. That makes obvious sense, but many managers, particularly those at the top, believe that they must exude a sense of continuous optimism, that leadership requires positive exaggeration and a rose-colored-glasses interpretation of every situation. Wrong. A company needs neither Pollyannas nor prophets of doom. It needs managers with down-to-earth realism who understand the world as it is, not as they would like it to be.

Employees are very savvy; they can quickly detect false optimism and unrealistic goals, even when couched in inspiring verbiage. A good manager must adopt a pragmatic philosophy about the outside factors not under his or her control. "What is, is." If one cannot change it or do something about it, one must accept it without likes or dislikes, emotions or tantrums. This attitude should apply to standing laws and regulations, minorities, religions, races, mores, habits, social behavior, politics, and weather.

The world of the future will be neither better nor worse; it will be different. Past experience becomes less and less valid and valuable. One must look at the future from an eyes-open perspective.

Are You Going in the Right Direction?

Use the following checklist of major changes in management trends, policies, and strategies to compare your relative position and current style with the overall direction of management thinking and implementation methods among today's corporate winners.

From	To
Organization	
Centralized (functional)	Decentralized (business units)
Hierarchical pyramid	Horizontal (fewer reporting layers)
Strong corporate staff services	Minimal central services
Planning	
Sequential planning process	Parallel/integrated planning process
Central direction and strategies	Decentralized planning (profit centers)
From top down	From grass roots up
Growth Policies	
Mass-market orientation	Niche (specialty) orientation
Market-share dominance	Item profitability evaluation
Unrelated diversification	Maintaining and protecting the golden goose

From	To
Acquisitions	Complementary mergers and acquisitions
Growth from within	Joint ventures (instant vertical integration)

Finances

Debt instruments	Equity instruments
Long-term financing (fixed rate)	Short-term financing (variable rate)
Selling stock	Buying stock back
P&L emphasis	Balance sheet and cash-flow emphasis
Stable foreign exchange	Unstable foreign exchange

Personnel

Generalists	Specialists
Organization cogs	Entrepreneurs/intrapreneurs
Dictatorial style	Participative, team management

Rewards

Stock options (long-term)	Immediate equity
Deferred compensation	Cash bonuses, profit sharing
Standardized benefits	Individualized, cafeteria-style benefits
Group, union contracts	Individual, nonunion accommodations

Marketplace

Local competition	Worldwide competition
National marketing programs	Regional, locally targeted programs
Product emphasis	Service and total system emphasis
Customer homogeneity	Customer pluralism, segmentation
Standardization (few choices)	Customization (many choices)
Emphasis on original equipment manufacturing (OEM)	After-market emphasis
Price orientation	Value orientation, quality image

From	To
Production	
Large manufacturing complexes	Small, flexible production units
Vertical integration	Subcontracting
Reliance on skilled labor	Robotics (labor elimination)
Large inventories	Just-in-time, zero inventories
Long runs	Customized short runs
U.S. production facilities	Offshore manufacturing and/or contracting
Data Processing / Communications	
Central data processing	Local, distributive data processing
CPU (batch) reliance	Terminal, real-time emphasis
Letters, reports, oral communications	Electronic data transmission, shared databases

And Don't Forget the Basics

Markets, customers, distribution channels, production methods, technology, and communications techniques may change; but certain basics of management do not change, nor should they be forgotten.

Peter Drucker is a master at reminding managers to deal with basics. Unless fundamentals are in place, no clever solution, no pioneering program, will withstand the forces of the external environment.

Drucker's definition of management is:

> *Effective and efficient use of available resources to achieve desired results.*

It may read like a generality, but it is basic truth. Every word should be analyzed, and the analysis should generate Monday morning actions.

- *"Effective."* Are all operations being performed on schedule and according to plan? Is the customer happy?
- *"Efficient."* Is the effectiveness profitable? Are costs under control? Are they correct?

- *"Available resources."* Have human and physical resources been analyzed carefully as to availability, performance, and cost? Could they be replaced by less costly or more up-to-date resources?
- *"Desired results."* What are they, precisely? Were objectives clearly analyzed and defined? Do they fit the situation?

The last factor—"desired results"—must be adapted to the company's outside-in strategy. Inside-out companies tend to stick stubbornly to their objectives despite changes in the external environment. But objectives should be relative, not absolute. They must be altered to fit the times.

At different periods, a company might choose any one of these overall objectives:

- *Supergrowth objectives* Sales growth, a race for bigness, market share, high leverage, high debt. Profits are expected to come later.
- *Earnings-per-share objectives* Stock market profits through high multiples. Quarter-by-quarter increase in earnings per share is essential to a high P/E ratio, but this is often to the detriment of the future because of delays in capital investment, shortcuts in maintenance, and neglect of R&D.
- *Return-on-investment objectives* Portfolio analysis, decisions made by pencil pushers looking at business as stock certificates, not as productive units of human and physical resources.
- *Cash-flow management objectives* Return to conservatism, low debt ratios, internal financing, low-risk investments.

None of these are good or bad objectives in themselves. But they must be decided upon and implemented to match the needs and forces of the external environment. As you sow, so shall you reap. Today's strategies, tomorrow's results.

Easy to say, difficult to do. But it must be done. That's why an outside-in strategy is so important. The recipe for success calls for common sense, objectivity, and willingness to adapt to change, mixed with sensitivity to early clues of change and the ability to respond with innovative action.

Monday Morning Actions

- Get started on building a sophisticated database for each of your markets, products, and services. Cheaper computer memories with faster access make such databases economically feasible. You should have complete histories, ordering patterns, likes and dislikes, even personalities of individual or classes of customers available, properly updated. Grass roots feedback is vital, because the way you think is not necessarily the way your consumers think. Take immediate steps to understand those consumers, so you can maintain a broad, balanced, and uninhibited perspective of the changing world and society. Thoughtful use of the information by all departments (not just marketing) will repay the effort many times over.
- Establish a continuous *formal* process for early recognition of clues to significant changes—which are really clues to problems and opportunities.
- List the many factors that are outside your control and may affect the company. Categorize and arrange these factors in order of how strong their impact on the business will be, whether positive or negative. Further analyze and refine the factors until they are reduced to five specific key external forces that you expect to be of utmost importance. (See Gap Analysis, Step 1, for more guidance on accomplishing this vital task.)
- Start paying attention to such platitudes as "determine your risk level," "watch your competition," and "keep your facilities up to date." If many top managements had heeded these bromides, they could have saved billions of dollars and millions of jobs.
- If necessary, get started on a major overhaul of your business unit's objectives, operations, and organization with the goal of creating a proactive organization that will anticipate and act upon changing external forces before they become obvious to others. The essential success factor today is the ability to make an early, accurate interpretation of changing demographic, economic, social, technological, political, and international forces.

PART THREE

Corporate Goals for 1993—Trigger Point Targets to Shoot for

TRIGGER POINT SIX

Raise productivity at least one and a half times higher than the real interest rate.

"The first test of management competence is productivity." PETER DRUCKER

Productivity improvement is crucial to every business. Familiar words. Unfortunately, this truism is often stated but equally often lacks top-priority commitment. But overall internal productivity increase *must* become one of the two most important objectives of your enterprise. (The other is customer demand.)

Your goal should be to raise productivity at least 1½ times higher than the *real* interest rate, that is, the prime rate minus the inflation rate. If the prime rate is 8.5 percent and the inflation rate is 1.5 percent, the real interest rate is 7 percent and you should aim to raise your productivity at least 10.5 percent.

In raising productivity, you should have three goals:

- Higher output (sales/units) per employee—greater labor productivity

- Higher capital/labor ratio—greater automation
- Lower break-even—greater flexibility and resilience for dealing with demand fluctuations.

We're in Deep Trouble

Overall U.S. productivity growth was once the world's highest. Now it's among the lowest: 1 percent. Time is running out for major decisions on changing this situation. We're closing in on the 1990s, and U.S. companies have not yet begun to boost productivity in earnest.

Here's what they face. Many other countries have invested in modern production facilities for heavy industry such as steel, aluminum, and petrochemicals. They've put money into the latest manufacturing and assembly techniques for motor vehicles, electronics, and machine tools. At the same time, their labor costs are considerably lower than in the United States. This combination of modern facilities and low labor costs creates a devastating competitive advantage and another new factor in the era of unpredictability. In the past the advantage was either modern plant and high labor cost (e.g., West Germany) or cheap labor and old facilities (e.g., Taiwan). That is no longer true.

The High Price of Arrogance

The chronic U.S. productivity gap didn't happen overnight; it grew over many decades. Increases in compensation per employee kept creeping ahead of real output per employee. The only reaction was to raise prices, resulting in an inflationary spiral that was aggravated but not totally caused by OPEC price increases during the 1970s. As other industrial countries became more prosperous and technologically independent, their output per employee grew at a much faster rate than that in the United States.

United States companies can't make the excuse that these countries started from a smaller base and that we modernized their production facilities after World War II. The war ended over 40 years ago; their "new" facilities have long since been obsolete. Moreover, the European Common Market now has a combined GNP larger than that of the United States.

The fact is that we have become complacent and arrogant. We ignored foreign progress and foreign competition for years until their impact hit like a ton of bricks. Between 1976 and 1986, the cumulative trade deficit was more than $650 billion—an immense outflow of funds, resources, and employment opportunities from the United States to the rest of the world. This affects our growth and our standard of living—and contributes to the federal deficit because of lower tax revenue.

This isn't leading to a soapbox plea for revival of national productivity; it's leading to a strong recommendation that individual companies make internal productivity a major strategic issue for very practical reasons:

1. Unless a United States–based company can compete with foreign imports, it will either go out of business or will have to move offshore, at least partially.
2. Sooner or later, large corporations will be forced, in self-defense, to invest in high-productivity programs. If they succeed, they'll become formidable competitors within the United States, and smaller U.S. companies that did not take action on this trigger point will fall on tough times.

Yes, Productivity Can *Be Revived*

There are simply no excuses for not implementing this trigger point. Productivity is an internal matter under full management control. Some may try to blame their productivity problems on external factors beyond their control such as unions and government regulations. Both excuses are smokescreens. Unions have become weaker, and the Reagan administration eased enforcement of regulations.

Let's take unions. The deep recession of 1982–1983 pushed unemployment to its highest levels since the Depression. An unemployment rate averaging 9.7 percent for 2 years shook the country and the union leadership. Organized labor was already weakening anyhow. Union membership began to shrink in 1977. By 1987, membership had dropped by 5 million and stood at its lowest level in two decades—at less than 18 percent of the work force.

There were many reasons. The structural change in manufacturing—particularly in smokestack industries—permanently eliminated the need for many unionized workers (automobiles, mining, steel). Labor force growth was among service workers: women, part-time help, white-collar employees, technical and professional people—not likely union prospects. Foreign competition and trade deficits cost the country over 1 million jobs. Much of the blame was laid on intransigent unions, whose policies and rules were hampering productivity. Several bankruptcies of major companies, partly due to noncompetitive labor costs, spurred deunionization (e.g., Continental Airlines). Major industries negotiated new contracts containing work rule concessions and pay rate reductions. Firms got tougher and kept operating successfully despite walkouts.

Times are changing. The union movement will continue to lose power. Contracts will be negotiated on a two-tier basis with much lower entry level hourly rates. Many impediments to automation and productivity improvements will fall. Executives will no longer be able to blame their low productivity and competitive disadvantage on the unions alone.

Where to Look. Productivity improvements can and should be sought in every activity of the enterprise. Purchasing can be smarter; deliveries can be made just-in-time. Reports can be timelier and more informative. Product development can be closer to the customer and be better attuned to the customer's needs. Materials handling can be more automated. Production can be scheduled more efficiently. Waste can be minimized. Personnel can be better motivated and trained. Preventive maintenance can be improved. Sales and marketing can be enhanced by new programs, conference sales calls, and remote demonstrations. Computers can be used more extensively for data analysis. Organization and reporting relationships can be changed for faster communications and faster decision making. We'll tell you how to develop next-Monday-morning actions to accomplish those goals. But first...

Boosting Productivity: There's a Right Way and a Wrong Way

M. Midas, Jr. and W. Werther have pointed out the pitfalls of *pseudo* productivity in the March 1985 issue of *Management Review*:

1. Too much reliance on cold financial data. The facts may tell what *is*, but not what *will be* or what to do about it. Chrysler's most profitable year was 1977. Two years later, it had to be bailed out by the federal government to survive.
2. End-of-the-month push that often produces two-thirds of monthly orders, resulting in higher costs and lower overall productivity. Crisis management is costly.
3. Overreliance on industrial engineering work measurement standards. Imposed standards seldom improve individual performance because they are ivory-tower-generated; there is no ownership of the goal.
4. Lack of security and real participation for many workers. Management policies and edicts are never fully implemented without the wholehearted participation of the ultimate implementers.
5. Productivity is seldom considered to be a major strategic issue that requires the CEO's continuous personal attention. How many companies have a senior VP in charge of productivity?

That last point is crucial. The three-legged stool of strategic management—market need, product and service, financial objectives—should have another leg: productivity improvement—continuously adding value to the company's output. This is essential in times of fast-changing technology, markets, and economic conditions. Market share gains in a mature industry lead to excess plant capacity and disastrous increases in fixed overhead. Look at steel, automobiles, rubber, shipbuilding. And, sadly, Caterpillar Tractor Company.

In 1978, Caterpillar was voted the best-managed company in the United States. Its giant yellow machines symbolized efficiency, quality, and service through its solid, profit-minded, no-nonsense management. With 35 percent of the world's market share and 50 percent of the U.S. share, it was rightly heralded as one of the best-run companies in the world.

Caterpillar strategy and implementation had a well-defined, steady direction:

- Very high quality products
- Fast premium service available everywhere
- Parts inventory of 25,000 items available within 24 hours anywhere in the world
- Premium price justified by super reputation and performance
- Excellent, large dealers: 93 in the United States and 137 abroad, covering 150 countries; happy, prosperous, dedicated
- Continuous large capital investments in modern computerized production plants
- Solid team management philosophy, low profile, no "stars" or personalities, no bureaucracy, small-company atmosphere, strong centralized production and financial controls
- Internal growth preferred to acquisitions
- High investment in R&D and product improvement

What Went Wrong? A single error destroyed Caterpillar's 48-year profit streak and shattered the illusion of invincibility. The company was not prepared for the extreme fluctuations of the 1980s. Rosy forecasts for 1982 were wrong. Major markets crumbled worldwide. Cat's $505 million acquisition of Solar Turbine from International Harvester was a masterpiece of mistiming. Overexpansion ($836 million on plants in 1981 alone) created a production capacity 100 percent above market demand. Losses during 1981 to 1984 exceeded $600 million. Debt soared from 20 to 40 percent of capitalization.

It all comes down to one basic failure: Caterpillar didn't realize that, in an unpredictable world, it should have pushed productivity up so it could push its break-even point down. As a result, it was sandbagged by the unexpected drop in world demand.

Cat has had to take drastic steps. It slashed costs, capital spending, R&D, and supervisory personnel. As of 1987, it had laid off

40 percent of its work force. It had to cut prices to fight competitive Komatsu. Caterpillar will rebound, in time, but will never be the same, because its management underestimated the magnitude and structure of global change. It did not adapt in time.

LOWER YOUR BREAK-EVEN!

Why are we using big type and an exclamation point? Because the single most practical, most effective way to deal with unpredictability, fluctuations, and fast obsolescence is to lower the corporation's break-even point in every business unit. The key management test is: Will the business break even when volume unexpectedly falls by 20 to 30 percent of normal? It's not an uncommon situation today and should be prepared for. On the positive side, low break-even provides high returns when business booms and permits additional flexibility for experimentation and innovation.

Case in Point: United States automobile makers had to reduce their break-even under fire. They were losing billions of dollars because of the recession and Japanese competition. Iacocca's biggest single achievement at Chrysler was to reduce the break-even by 50 percent and realize the highest profits in the entire history of Chrysler at half the sales volume. General Motors' worldwide employment rose only 5.2 percent in 1983 while unit production increased 24 percent, a productivity increase of 18 percent. Its dollar sales rose 24 percent with costs up only 17 percent.

The same is true of Ford. In 1984, it completed the most profitable year in its history, 4 years after posting its biggest loss of $1.5 billion in 1980. It achieved this by cutting $4.5 billion in operating costs over 5 years. White-collar employment was permanently cut by 30 percent. Net result: Ford lowered its break-even point in North American operations by 40 percent.

These achievements may seem less spectacular when you consider that U.S. automobile makers were fat, inefficient, backward, and arrogant. But so are many other enterprises.

Lesson to Be Learned

Unfortunately, the frequent response to profit-margin erosion is not to reduce the break-even, but to abandon the low-end market and move higher and higher into expensive, sophisticated products. Xerox used this short-sighted, head-in-sand approach when it abandoned the small-copier field to the Japanese. When he became Xerox CEO after this move, David Kearns reported: "We learned that our costs were not only way out in left field, they weren't even in the ballpark. We were horrified to find that the Japanese were *selling* their small machines for what it cost us to *make* ours—their selling price equaled our manufacturing costs!"

What You Must Do to Lower Your Break-Even

Lowering the break-even point requires six major thrusts:

- *Maximum automation.* That means fully using commercially available new technology, machinery, tools, robots, materials handling conveyors, automatic devices. Invest serious amounts of capital to modernize the facilities to the fullest. The depreciation on investment plus the labor savings add to flexibility and reduce the break-even (contrary to the conventional wisdom of the green-eyeshade pencil pushers).
- *Smaller labor force.* The number of employees must be cut: blue-collar workers through automation, white-collar workers through computers and reorganization. Shift labor-intensive operations overseas.
- *Higher labor productivity.* Proper training and motivation will boost the productivity of remaining employees. Pay them more, commensurately with their performance.
- *Integrated computer system.* Integrate the entire company through use of terminals, communications, and shared databases. This will achieve major efficiency gains.
- *Hands-on organization.* Eliminating many middle-management layers will increase direct communications and involvement. The result: a faster, better decision-making and execution process.

- *Better methods.* Example: The just-in-time (JIT) inventory control system. When properly used, it can sharply reduce inventory costs in capital, control, and space.

Let's explore these six imperatives.

Automation: Some of Our Best Friends Are Robots

A GE executive summarizes the alternatives facing many U.S. companies: "Automate, emigrate, or evaporate." Factory automation could reverse the deindustrialization trend. The technology is available, but U.S. companies are dragging their feet.

For the new future, the essential form of automation is robotics or "intelligent" machines—equipment with multiple sensory abilities under computer control. The Japanese are leading in this field. While U.S. robot production increased 25 percent, Japan's went up 80 percent. Japan has 120,000 robots and the United States has 15,000, with other countries trailing far behind. West Germany and Sweden are producing and installing robots at a fast pace, but starting from a small base. Most U.S. robots are in auto plants; in Japan the robots are in electrical or electronic equipment production.

Advantages of Robots

1. Robots facilitate competition with low-wage countries by reducing labor content. Semiconductor production is moving back to the United States and Japan from Taiwan and Korea.
2. They are recession-resistant because they can lower break-even to 40 to 65 percent of capacity.
3. They reduce barriers to entry by allowing small companies to compete with biggies—robots require relatively small capital investment for the performance. Rather than being immense machines that cost $10 million, they are basically in the $50,000-to-$100,000 range.
4. They increase manufacturing flexibility. Plant locations don't de-

pend on labor availability. Fast setup facilitates fast turnaround time, making smaller lots economical. New-model start-up is greatly accelerated.

Disadvantages of Robots

Robotics requires careful preparation, training, and motivation of employees in a new work environment. There's also the problem of transferring and utilizing displaced personnel. But isn't it both economically and humanely better to lay off 20 percent of workers and continue in business than to close down operations altogether?

Manufacturing Flexibility Is the Key

Factories must be more flexible because mass production is dying out. Huge assembly lines are out of date. Cars, cameras, and candlesticks now come in small batches. Three-quarters of all machined parts in the world are produced in lots of 50 or less.

Factories must learn to cope with batch production. Here are the technologies that will help:

- *Computer-aided design (CAD).* Companies using CAD systems generate unidimensional product designs 3 to 6 times faster than before. Chrysler says it takes them 30 minutes to make drawings that took 3 months by hand. The next step is for CADs to work with solid models and generate accurate three-dimensional machining instructions. Solid-modelers are being perfected, and costs are coming down within the reach of smaller companies.
- *Computer-aided engineering (CAE).* This system will verify plans and quality and design molds and tools.
- *Computer-aided manufacturing (CAM).* CAM will send operating signals to computer-controlled machine tools, computer-aided assemblies (CAA), and other robots, including automated materials handling and automated warehouses. Already, computerized management systems plan and schedule production, check consumption, and keep track of inventories. Data are fed

to and received from purchasing, finance, marketing, and all related functions.

- *Computer-integrated manufacturing (CIM).* CIM will allow any U.S. manufacturer to compete favorably with offshore factories. It requires automating and linking all factory functions and headquarters operations.
- *Flexible manufacturing system (FMS).* A miniature version of CIM, FMS can be installed by smaller manufacturers with an investment of $5 million.

Flexibility costs money, but it's vital. Money must be found and spent, or there will be no business. The costs are much smaller than those for a large assembly plant of the past. Thus, smaller companies can become efficient suppliers or OEMs. The main advantage of flexible manufacturing is not in labor saving, but in inventory saving and the ability to produce small batches to customers' specs rapidly and profitably.

Monday Morning Actions

- If you are a U.S. manufacturer, accumulate knowledge not just on your world competitors, but on the latest available software and hardware methods of modern production.
- Prepare a long-range plan for modernization of your production. Base it on faster throughput, lower inventories, flexible batch production, ability to customize, greater facility utilization.
- Calculate the capital necessary to achieve the revitalization or major improvement of your manufacturing operations.
- Prepare a comprehensive prospectus to raise the necessary funds.

Lower Your Break-Even through Work Force Reductions

Some companies call it downsizing, some RIF (reduction in force). But whatever it's called, there is a major trend toward reducing work forces. Fortune 500 companies have 2.2 million fewer employees than in 1979. GE laid off 90,000; Exxon, 40,000; AT&T, 37,000; DuPont, 16,000; Bank of America, 10,000; Kodak, 24,000. Chrysler cut 50 percent of its salaried employees. Large industrials reduced their middle- and upper-level management by 600,000. GM and Ford plan to keep reducing white-collar jobs by 5 percent a year. Smaller companies also are getting into the act.

This is only the beginning of a serious effort to streamline U.S. operations, eliminate overhead, and become fast, fluid, and flexible. Work forces are reduced through automation, subcontracting, and worldwide manufacturing and sourcing. White-collar jobs are trimmed through data processing and electronic communications, consolidation of operations, and determined pruning of nonessential functions.

Altogether, some 24 million jobs have been lost but replaced. The major shift was from manufacturing to services, from mature industries to electronics and high tech. The trend will continue, but the economy will be able to absorb massive relocations because of a drop in labor force growth. "Baby bust"—a decline of the birth rate since the 1960s—will reduce the overall labor growth between 1987 and 1995 to 1.1 percent, down from 2.5 percent in the 1970s.

Monday Morning Actions

- Continue reduction of work force by automating operations in every phase of your activities from factory to tellers' windows.
- Concentrate on streamlining middle-management personnel. Replace messengers (production schedulers, inventory clerks, order processors) with electronic communications.
- Establish an orderly reduction of personnel through attrition, voluntary separations, and early retirements.
- Reorganize and upgrade your personnel department to handle knowledge workers. Emphasis must be on quality rather than on quantity of output; on work flow, job design, and job relations rather than on traditional training; on talent and motivation rather than on bargain pay.

- Establish "parallel ladders" of advancement, pay, and opportunity for many valuable professionals who do not want to be managers.

Achieve Higher Labor Productivity through Motivation

Motivating employees is certainly not a new topic. Literally tons of material have been published about it. Still, it is the most neglected, misunderstood, and mismanaged part of business operations in most companies, large or small, here or abroad. How many companies do you know that pay all of their employees a yearly bonus that effectively doubles their pay and have done so since the late 1930s? There is only one in the United States: Lincoln Electric Company of Cleveland, established in 1896. Its productivity record is unique and surely worth a careful analysis. What's behind it?

- Written guaranteed employment of a minimum 30 hours a week; no layoffs in over 40 years.
- No mandatory retirement; employees can collect retirement pay *and* paychecks.
- Yearly bonus based on ideas and cooperation, output, work quality, and ability to work with no supervision. (The supervisor/employee ratio is 1:100.)
- Self-motivation principle that allows employees to rearrange and restructure their work.
- Meager benefits, no executive perks, no breaks, no base pay, all compensation based on piecework incentive and production output.
- Employee-elected advisory board that meets twice monthly.
- Open-door policy.
- No outside hiring except at entry level.
- Japanese-style *kamban* "just-in-time" inventory system, practiced for over 35 years without any central stockroom.

Opinions of the Lincoln Electric system range from one extreme to another. Norman Berg, professor of business administration at Harvard, studied Lincoln for years. He maintains that many companies could greatly profit from adopting the Lincoln process. In contrast, Robert Guest, professor of organizational behavior at Dartmouth, believes that Lincoln's environment is unique and that its system could not be successfully transferred to any other organization. Whatever the academicians say, only results count and Lincoln Electric is performing exceptionally well. It is worth investigating.

A Tale of Two Ford Plants. The Ford Motor plants in Saarlouis, West Germany, and Halewood, England, are identical in capacity, layout, and equipment. But the West German plant's 7762 workers produce 1200 cars a day, while the 10,040 British workers produce under 800. The net productivity of the West German worker is twice that of the British: 21 man-hours per car versus 40. True, the German workers average $13.50 an hour compared with the British workers' $8.25. But the pay differential is irrelevant. British Ford management would be happy to match the German pay if worker productivity were on the same level. The problem is not pay, but motivation. In the Halewood plant, it's a continuous battle between management and the union. Halewood has established new records for sabotage, strikes (20 in one year), man-hours lost, miserable quality (14 percent rejects vs. 1 percent in Saarlouis), and sales revenue losses (some $800 million in 5 years).

Matsushita of Japan had a better idea when it acquired Quasar from Motorola. Quasar was a moribund TV set operation in Franklin Park, Illinois. Matsushita inherited a mess consisting of yearly warranty bills of $22 million, a defect rate of 140 for every 100 TV sets, complaints from 70 percent of customers within 90 days of sale, and a personnel turnover of 30 percent.

Progress was not instantaneous, but, within 5 years of Japanese-style management in the United States, warranty costs were down to $3.5 million, defects were down to 6 per 100 TV sets, complaints were down to 7 percent of buyers, and turnover of the same labor pool was down to 1 percent. It took a lot of retraining and motivating of over 1000 workers—who ended up with a new sense of pride and belonging. Better direct communication was probably the key ingredient; it was achieved by cutting middle-management positions down to 300 from 600.

What Does Motivation Require? A productivity-oriented organization does not play games or manipulate people. The people have become too smart to buy that. The organization needs a sincere and honest leadership, two-way communication, non–Mickey Mouse programs, cooperative efforts, delegation, participation, and teamwork. Those may sound like pious platitudes, but they are the only ways to motivate with lasting results. One giant that is making good (but still embryonic) progress in this direction is Ford Motor Company. It is obviously easier in smaller organizations. That explains the push for independent, self-sufficient business units and flat, horizontal, entrepreneurial organizations. The days of large and powerful central staffs are numbered. This is the era of participative leaders and grass roots doers. There is no place for middle-management empires, bureaucracy, and buffer zones.

Motivation requires you to educate your workers. You need to communicate with them. You really have to understand them. Ask yourself, how do I motivate my people to be (*a*) productive directly and (*b*) effective with the customer? Either you are going to motivate or you are not going to have the lowest break-even point and you are not going to have customer satisfaction. Motivation is the difference.

Basically, to motivate people in today's society, you should ask each employee, "What do you want?" Unfortunately, personnel departments try to treat everybody the same. That means treating everybody at an equal level of mediocrity—and making them unhappy. But today is a new era. We have a pluralistic society in which everyone wants to be different. Women don't want to be like men; men don't want to be like women; blacks don't want to be like whites; the old don't want to be treated like the young; the young don't want to be treated like the old. We have a segmented-subculture society.

That means we must motivate people as individuals. Ask people what they want and create a cafeteria-style benefit program by which the same $500 or $1000 may be used differently for each individual. It is a more difficult approach that is scorned by pencil-pushing bureaucrats; but it makes a substantial difference in motivating employees, so it is worth doing. You can have a vibrant organization rather than a mediocre organization. This is basically the secret (if there is a secret) of being more productive.

One mistake to avoid: emphasizing profit to motivate the employee. Don't say, "We must make a profit, so you must work more productively." What does one of the 220,000 employees of DuPont care about DuPont's profit? Nothing. The employee's reaction is, "What is it? *I* never see it. It doesn't do *me* any good, why do they keep on talking about *their* profit?" Take "profit" out of your vocabulary. Instead, try talking to each employee about what he or she can accomplish personally.

Monday Morning Actions

- Appoint a very talented and respected individual to report directly to the CEO and to be in charge of an overall annual productivity (value-added) improvement of *x* percent. Every department and every individual must make a quantitative commitment to measurably contribute to achieving that goal. This Operation Stretch must bring about results above and beyond the business-as-usual yearly budgets and operating plans. You will be amazed by the results your organization can achieve.

Integrate Your Operations through Computerization

We require higher internal productivity to cope with leapfrog advances in technology and global competition. Since most management functions are based on communications, the essential first step is to establish a network of terminals available to managers for electronic exchange of common data and for individual analysis and manipulation of the information.

Why is this so vital? Quite suddenly, in the late 1970s, a new era dawned: the age of information. It was made possible by the explosion of electronics and computer and communications technology. The new era is still in its infancy, but its prospects are extraordinary. Executives must deliberately shed their past experience and habits to adapt to the remarkable new opportunities to help them operate their businesses more productively.

During a 30-year period, the price of computation was reduced by a factor of 700; and in the next few years, that extraordinary progress was doubled. For example, between 1965 and 1987, optical character recognition equipment allowing direct input of printed material to computer memory, in digital and retrievable form, decreased in cost from about $1 million to about $2000. The significance of this new price ratio to information management is enormous.

But despite these revolutionary hardware and cost benefits, the productivity of the U.S. manager did not rise commensurably. An executive typically devotes 94 percent of the workday to communications-related activities. Oral communications are 69 percent (53 percent face-to-face and 16 percent by telephone). Written communications take 25 percent of the time. That leaves 6 percent of the time for the primary executive duties: problem solving, conceptualizing, and long-range planning.

The opportunity for productivity increases is immense, but progress is very slow. Office workers will soon comprise 55 percent of the U.S. work force. Office costs constitute some 40 to 50 percent of total business expense. United States business has some 320 billion *paper* documents on file—an average of five filing cabinets per worker—and one-third of the files are never retrieved.

The manager must also spend time and effort to learn useful analytical techniques for making better use of available information. A new, more structured discipline of communications will have to be accepted by all the people linked by the network. They particularly will have to change their meeting habits. Meetings are increasing in number and duration. They are costly, particularly when travel is involved ($350 billion is spent annually on travel-related expenses). The new society and new technology require new, fresh personal approaches. The executive must show a determination to embrace these opportunities with enthusiasm, not with reluctance, and to lead others in rapidly adapting to change.

Telecommuting. Here's a way to utilize new information technology to increase productivity. Telecommuting—working at home, while linked to one's office through electronics—is already a reality. A Minneapolis computer company has 70 employees working at home. An insurance company in Little Rock has 20 clerks processing entries at home. They enjoy the flexibility; they are able to tend to their home chores; and their productivity has soared. Also, their work is more easily measured and controlled.

A creative individual in Steamboat Springs, Colorado, is happily working for a California outfit. He didn't want to leave his picturesque village, and the company did not have to finance a costly move. A New York stockbroker can work at home better than in the office and have equal facilities to serve his customers. He saves 3 hours of hectic commuting each day; he saves thousands of dollars on transportation and meals; and he has a tax deduction for his at-home office expenses.

Employers gain by saving on expensive office space. Obviously, not everyone can or should telecommute. But a variety of solitary, task-oriented work can be efficiently performed this way.

What's Coming. The use of sophisticated communications will grow. Executives will increasingly turn to video teleconferencing because it is more practical and less costly than many present junkets. Portable terminals will be used extensively by salespeople and technicians during their customer calls to create direct links with their home offices (for orders or diagnoses). Cars equipped with computers hooked up to cellular phones will further add to the mobility and flexibility of communications. The list of possibilities can go on and on. The technology is exploding, and costs are plummeting.

Monday Morning Actions

- Become computer-literate. Keep up-to-date on the latest electronic developments; learn to operate terminals and access databases. Use a small computer yourself, daily. Get familiar with the systems architecture of your new tools linking voice, data, graphics, documents, and images into an integrated network to make a quantum jump in managerial efficiency.
- Start networking within your organization. Link various departments and operations to common or shared databases.

- Expand the electronic links to your field operations, key customers, and key suppliers.
- Do it gradually but steadily, on a predetermined plan and schedule—and stick to it.
- Do it even if you're not a biggie. Businesses with fewer than 25 employees are successfully networking their internal operations and electronically ordering from suppliers.

Hands-on Management Is Essential—We Have Too Many Layers!

Three very efficient organizations in the world have just 5 levels of management; GM has 18. The three with five layers are Honda, Toyota, and the Catholic Church.

I am not saying everyone should go to five levels. I am saying reduce what you have. Consider the organization of most of your biggies: at top, the board of directors, the chairman of the board, the chief executive officer, and the chief of operations. Then you have some executive vice presidents, and they have a few senior vice presidents, who have a few group vice presidents, who have a few vice presidents. Finally, on the seventh level there is somebody who does some work.

There's a billion dollar company in England with a CEO who has a staff of 36. He has 80 presidents of divisions reporting directly to him. Can that work? Yes, but there are two things you must have. Number one, the 80 people must be very good. If you have 80 dummies reporting to you, you will go crazy talking to them all. So you need 80 motivated, very intelligent people: entrepreneurs. You don't need a big staff to keep them informed; if you have a shared database and you are computerized, you can keep them informed by pressing buttons.

Striking the Right Chord. Peter Drucker is without doubt the foremost management scholar in the world. Not only has he maintained that post for the past 40 years; he continually adds new concepts and innovative ideas to keep ahead of the fast-changing social and economic environment. His June 4, 1985, article in *The*

Wall Street Journal, "Playing in the Information-Based Orchestra," was, in my opinion, so outstanding that it should be on the must-read list of every business executive.

Drucker contends that the business organization should be restructured around the flow of information. " The information-based structure is 'flat,' with far fewer levels of management." Automated manufacturing plants could dispense with most of the traditional layers between the plant manager and the first-line supervisors. In some actual cases, up to 7 out of 12 layers were cut out. They were not levels of authority or decision making; they were merely relays or buffers for information dissemination. The classical principle of span of control (upper limit of six subordinates to report to one superior) is made obsolete by a new principle of "span of communications." The number of reporting personnel is limited only by their "willingness to take responsibility for their own communications and relationships, upward, sideways, and downward." Control becomes the ability to obtain information.

Drucker makes a further important point: An "information-based organization does not actually require advanced information technology. All it requires is willingness to ask: Who requires what information, when and where?"

The flat organization permits and uses many more specialists: technicians, specific marketeers, designated customer representatives, quality-assurance experts. They all work together and separately, united by common information, but without the bureaucratic, stifling, hierarchical reporting links. The concept melds "purely managerial units, charged with optimizing what exists, and entrepreneurial units, charged with making obsolete what exists and with creating a different tomorrow."

The difference between a traditional command authority and the information-based management is in the direction of information flow. In the past, it was mainly from the top down; now it has become truly circular through the new organization. Peter Drucker's metaphor for this flat organization is the symphony orchestra.

"The conventional organization of business was originally modeled after the military. The information-based system much more closely resembles the symphony orchestra. All instruments play the same score. But each plays a different part. They play together, but they rarely play in unison." Drucker also makes the point that the violins are not the bosses of the horns, or vice versa. Even the first violin does not give orders to the second or third.

There is a difference, however. The orchestra has a written score that is given in advance to the conductor and the players. A business does not have the luxury of such precision. It obviously needs objectives and strategies that are agreed upon in advance, but the implementation may change as operations and events unfold.

"The information-based organization is not permissive; it is disciplined," declares Drucker. "It requires strong, decisive leadership." Great orchestra conductors are very demanding. They are perfectionists with rare abilities to coach, to make even the "junior" instruments perform admirably. The information-based organization requires "leadership that respects performance but demands self-discipline and upward responsibility from the first-level supervisor all the way to top management."

Monday Morning Actions

- Analyze your organization, its reporting functions, its flow of information, its control system, its players. Could it be restructured according to Drucker's information-based orchestra concept? I believe it could, successfully. Try it.

Get Me to the Line on Time: A Better Approach to Inventory Control

Tons of material have been written about the *kamban* just-in-time system of inventory control. Yet there is more talk and misunderstanding than action. The system was developed in the early 1950s by Toyota. A *kamban* is a job instruction chart showing what parts are needed: when, where, and how many. Workers or suppliers in early stages produce only what the *kamban* says and give it to the assembly workers just-in-time. Skillful use of *kamban* can produce remarkable productivity results: Stocks of parts and goods in process are cut to almost zero; inventory costs in capital, control, and space are sharply reduced.

But improper management of *kamban* will wreak chaos in production and can ruin a company. The keys to success are:

- Quality production. Preassembly stages must supply no defective parts.
- Punctuality. Parts must arrive on time.
- Coordination. The assembly line must collect and use the parts as scheduled.

These prerequisites are difficult enough when you're dealing with your own employees. They become even more difficult when you're dealing with hundreds of suppliers. Inevitable revisions in production schedules must be handled directly by the workers and supervisors, through personal communication and mutual understanding. Japanese companies endured big problems for years before the system really worked. Toyota took 13 years to hone it to near-perfection. But now the company considers the investment, the training, and the supplier network to be an "invisible" management resource that creates superior performance.

Keep in mind that the same long-term effort was required to install and perfect *value analysis* (VA). Although developed in the United States for cost reduction without volume increase, it was embraced by Hitachi in 1967, combined with quality circles, and worked on for 7 years before remarkable results started emerging: costs cut annually by 5 to 6 percent of sales for the next 10 successive years.

United States managers trying to install a just-in-time system find it's tough to break away from the old system. A stockroom full of parts and other inventory represents a security blanket. It also covers a multitude of errors in quality control, production scheduling, equipment failures, wrong or delayed deliveries from suppliers, and other "normal" daily occurrences. One suddenly has to trust the suppliers to deliver the right goods at the right time. The first tendency is to shift the inventory to the supplier. "Let them keep it in stock and ship when we need it." Xerox tried that and paid dearly for its ineptness. Be prepared for a long period of training, cooperation, and mutual learning before a just-in-time system really works.

To make it work, a company must reorganize production and firm up order schedules to allow suppliers to plan better. Train-the-trainers classes must be started so suppliers can teach their own people to set up similar systems. Company buyers and engineers must spend time at the supplier facilities to simplify and improve designs, reduce setup time, and provide greater flexibility. Quality being essential, workers should be taught statistical analysis so they can detect early changes in the performance of their equipment. The supplier must become a team member and has to be treated that way. Eventually, the suppliers should be reduced in number, preferably to those closest to the main plant. Under proper incentives and fair contracts, some suppliers are willing to move closer.

The just-in-time system can perform magnificently: 30 to 40 percent cost savings. But to make it succeed, you must:

- Carefully study and analyze the experiences of others: Toyota, Hitachi, Xerox, Hewlett-Packard, Harley-Davidson.
- Be prepared for years of continuous work and attention to effect change and improvement.
- Train and help suppliers as much as your own people. Treat them as partners, not slaves.
- Persevere, despite all the difficulties, or you will not remain competitive in this tough environment.

How Do You Measure Productivity?

Productivity is what you get out for what you put in. The classical overall formula is:

$$\text{Productivity} = \frac{\text{total output (revenue)}}{\text{total input}}$$

To be meaningful, however, it should be further categorized into productivity of labor, materials, capital, and markets. Although all these elements are basic and essential to the success of any business, very few companies make systematic, organized productivity efforts guided by consistent productivity measurements and controls. Does your company have an officer specifically in charge of productivity and nothing else?

Strategic thinkers increasingly are turning toward *value added* as the most appropriate measurement of output for each independent business unit. Value added is the difference between the market price of products and services sold and the company's cost of purchasing materials and services contained in the final sale. It separates what a business does from what its suppliers and customers do. It applies to all types of businesses and to all segments of a multiproduct-service corporation.

Value added has several important, yet subtle, nuances:

- Adding or reducing costs is not automatically reflected in corresponding value added. The customer and the market always have the last say in their valuations of a company's pricing policies.
- Value added is the only (except for equity) source of funds to finance the operations.
- Unlike standard costs and unit volumes, value added takes into account uncertainty, change, and customer perception of value—all of which are important considerations in today's environment.

Measurements. Several ratios are useful for strategic analysis of business productivity trends over a period of time. But make certain that all calculations are made in real terms, and adjust all monetary values to inflation by selecting one common base year and the appropriate deflator index. The following measurement categories are considered basic:

$$\text{Personnel productivity} = \frac{\text{real value added}}{\text{employees (or categories of employees)}}$$

$$\text{Resource productivity} = \frac{\text{real value added}}{\text{units of key resource (critical use)}}$$

$$\text{Capital productivity} = \frac{\text{real value added}}{\text{real investment}}$$

$$\text{Market productivity} = \frac{\text{operating profit}}{\text{value added}}$$

These categories can be further subdivided into finer cuts and measurements of specific items. The purpose of preparing and looking at the various current and historical ratios is to manage value added, not just to manage costs. The difference is great and the task is more difficult because each involves factors not under the company's control, such as market price acceptance.

The basic message is that a successful business must add genuine value in its resale to the customer. A combination of good value, fair price, and low costs will result in continuing growth and profits. It's obviously easier said than done. Kodak's policy of just sticking its label on Matsushita's videocassettes, Canon's copiers, and Dysan's floppy disks violates value-added parameters and will probably make these "new" businesses a resounding flop. ComputerLand, Inc. and many of its 800 franchised independent stores are undergoing a major value-added crisis. Operating cost reductions and fights over the structure of commissions are Band-Aids that will not stop massive hemorrhaging caused by major structural market change: shift in customer demand (from individual to business), fierce competition among hardware suppliers, and cutthroat price discounts, combined with customers' disillusionment over unfulfilled "full service" promises. In both cases, value-added analysis would be very beneficial and revealing.

Monday Morning Actions

- Prepare a separate productivity analysis for every business center using the value-added concept. Do it in real terms over the period of the past 5 years; look at concrete, meaningful segments of manpower, materials, capital, and markets. If this is properly executed, the conclusions will jump at you. They can then become a solid base for an effort to produce new thinking and suggest innovative actions.

Summing Up: A Productivity Action Plan

A company determined to improve its overall productivity dramatically should initiate serious, simultaneous drives in three directions.

A. *Commitment to latest commercially available technology*
   1. Computers
      Shorten time between innovation and commercialization (e.g., CAD-CAM, market database).
      Automate cost- and time-consuming clerical tasks (e.g., insurance policies, automatic teller machines, paperless factory at the Tandem company).
      Improve and speed up communications (electronic mail, shared database, telecommuting).
      Install computer-integrated manufacturing (CIM) for total production overview and planning (e.g., MRPII systems).
      Extend CIM to CIC (computer-integrated company).
   2. Robotics
      Automate wherever possible.
      Eliminate manual tasks with multipurpose, programmable machines (e.g., Unimation, Asea, GMFanuc, IBM).
      Work toward payout in 2 to 2½ years.
   3. Energy
      Reduce energy use by conservation, recycling, different sources, new processes, better monitoring.

B. *Commitment to greater investment in R&D*
   1. Allocate more resources (a higher percentage of sales) to internal R&D.
   2. Monitor worldwide R&D trends relevant to your business.
   3. Look for licenses and joint ventures that will enhance your innovation posture.

C. *Commitment to better, more efficient labor utilization*
   1. Cut staff personnel, clerical workers, and middle management by computer emphasis.
   2. Cut bottom-tier workers by robotics and automation emphasis.
   3. Train, motivate, and reward your experienced, skilled, key personnel.
   4. Seek genuine labor-management cooperation to achieve flexibility (multitask assignments), innovation (quality circles), accountability (delegate responsibility to lowest levels).
   5. Establish a flat, horizontal organization based on profit centers and business units.

TRIGGER POINT SEVEN

Beat your competition by 10 percent.

"The imagination is the power of the mind over the possibilities of things."
WALLACE STEVENS

Beat your competition by 10 percent—that's a goal every business should strive for. It's not necessary to obliterate your competition. That can only be done by a company with deep pockets—the capability to outlast your opposition in an all-out price war. That's the way the major airlines killed People Express when it began to annoy them, but only a few giants are in a position to win that kind of war.

To beat their competition today, smart companies must focus on segments of the increasingly pluralistic marketplace and develop products and services that have unique characteristics based on quality, patents, delivery, charisma, integrity, or financing—characteristics that permit them to compete on *value,* not price. They must expand their support for existing product lines through repair services, preventive maintenance, planned replacement, leasing arangements, operating arrangements, and customer training.

They must develop innovative, rifle-shot marketing strategies that aim directly at a specific segment of the consumer population. They must look for niches in which they can exploit 90 percent of 1 percent of a market. They must *build* quality into their products instead of trying to "inspect" it in—and deliver quality service that's at least 10 percent better than the competition.

The Price of Staying in Business Is Eternal Innovation

To succeed today, every business needs innovation with the goal of creating uniqueness. This need is created by three major factors:

1. *Faster-changing technology.* Innovation is required to keep existing products and services from becoming obsolete because of rapidly occurring technological breakthroughs.
2. *Faster market saturation.* Better mass distribution and communication speed up the offering of products and services to the entire market (often worldwide), while consumer and commercial credit provide more immediate buying power. This creates a need to provide innovative new products and services at shorter intervals.
3. *Faster competition.* The pioneer's time advantage is shrinking. Competitors—who don't incur the high R&D costs which must be amortized by the innovator—are close behind. P&G's soft-cookie breakthrough was copied within 6 months by Nabisco and others. Sony and IBM are in trouble because their premium-price innovations are duplicated in months by at least half a dozen imitators at discount rates. This means that companies cannot simply rest on their laurels after innovating a new product or service; they must *constantly* innovate.

Uniqueness does not apply only to a product or service. You can develop uniqueness in every aspect of a business; for example:

- *Marketing.* Instead of selling its plastic housewares in stores, Tupperware innovated by selling through Tupperware parties held in people's homes.

- *Production.* Canon developed one of the world's most automated assembly systems to make its cameras—and cut its defect rate to virtually zero.
- *Personnel.* Lincoln Electric motivates its employees with a unique incentive-pay system.
- *Organization.* RTZ of UK, Baker International (now Baker Hughes) in the United States, and Toyota, in Japan, have moved to "flat" or "horizontal" organizations. They've cut out layers of reporting levels by delegating responsibility and accountability down the line. GE has followed suit. Mohasco cut corporate staff from more than 700 to 40 over 10 years by transferring centralized functions to divisions. Advantages: faster communications, better local decisions, faster implementation.
- *Joint ventures.* Can't beat the Japanese? Then, join them! Automotive: GM-Toyota, Ford-Mazda, Chrysler-Mitsubishi. Computers: Honeywell-NEC, National Semiconductor–Hitachi, Amadahl-Fujitsu.

In each example, innovation provides a competitive advantage—that 10 percent edge.

Ask any CEO to describe the uniqueness of that company's operations. If you get a quick, specific answer, the company is in good shape. If there is hesitation, the uniqueness may not be so unique. If there is a deafening silence, that company is in trouble.

There's More than One Road to Uniqueness

—and innovators are always looking for them. Examples:

IBM's Rental Innovation

In 1916, Thomas Watson, Jr., asked the Morgan Guaranty Trust for a small loan for the fledgling company he called IBM. He did not give the usual bromides about providing a useful service with quality equipment at fair prices to a large market. What he said was that he would not sell the equipment, he would rent it for the economic value of the service. This was a revolutionary concept for the times.

Xerox's Price per Copy Innovation

Fifty years later, Xerox—then Haloid—also needed financing. It did not use IBM's rental approach, because that was no longer unique. It innovated with price per copy. This "simple" concept became a winner and spurred the early supergrowth of Xerox. (Twenty-five years later, Xerox forgot the definition of innovation when it established computer retail stores after the market had already been preempted by Computerland, IBM, and others. Lacking uniqueness, the program was a costly failure.)

3M's Post-It™ Innovation

A few years ago, the 3M Company demonstrated a pad of little yellow note pages, each with a sticky strip so it could be attached to correspondence and later be easily removed. One consultant thought it was an asinine idea and was priced too high to sell. But it became the company's hottest seller and grossed more than $250 million in 1986. Rumor has it that this product was developed as the result of a failure. 3M engineers were trying to develop a superglue. One of their experimental formulas did not stick very well and seemed to have little use—until someone said: "Let's use it to make small, sticky yellow pads."

Coleco's Doll Innovation

Coleco could have gone bankrupt when its Adam home computer died as a $400 million flop. But Coleco had a magic backup: the Cabbage Patch doll. Although Coleco did not originate adoption certificates for dolls, it had the creative intuition to buy the concept from the small artist-producer who had invented it. That intuition was worth $500 million.

How to Acquire Uniqueness

You can acquire uniqueness—or in marketing language, *major positive differentiation*—in several ways. Uniqueness can be:

- *Scientifically researched.* New products through R&D, market niches through demographic studies, pricing innovation through simulation, incentives and motivation through behavior surveys.

- *Adapted.* Worldwide studies of kindred operations in noncompetitive areas may yield worthwhile results.
- *Acquired.* Patents, licenses, and businesses are available if the price is right.
- *Created.* Creating innovation internally is probably the best approach, but there are no formulas for doing it successfully. It requires a combination of two ingredients: creative talent and a supportive environment. It also requires a determination to put the word "uniqueness" at the forefront of one's thinking and sweat through the process of Monday morning actions focused on one goal: beating the competition by 10 percent.

Obviously, uniqueness can originate anywhere, and it needn't be complex. But it must be recognized and exploited to gain that 10 percent edge on the competition. A deep need exists for an atmosphere that encourages entrepreneurship, innovation, creativity, and risk taking, all the way to the marketplace.

The three cases that follow provide vivid proof that it can be done.

A "Ridiculous" Idea That Made Millions

Federal Express is a striking example of how innovative adaptation can give you the uniqueness needed to beat the competition. For years, airlines have utilized the hub concept, bringing passengers to a major metropolitan center and flying them out to their destinations. The founder of Federal Express thought to duplicate the hub concept for the air delivery of packages. He first described this idea in a college thesis. His professor gave him a mark of C-minus and commented that the concept was completely unworkable and didn't make sense.

He ran into the same reaction when he tried to start a business based on his concept. Conventional wisdom rejected the practicality of shipping a package from San Francisco to Los Angeles by flying it at night to Memphis, Tennessee, and then air-freighting it immediately back to Los Angeles.

But it worked. Within a few years, Federal Express was a billion dollar giant, still gathering millions of packages every day and night in Memphis and distributing them all around the country. Nobody laughs at the founder any more; he paid himself a bonus of over $50 million and deserved every million of it.

Of course, having or adapting an idea is not enough. Solid implementation must follow. Federal Express has pioneered in the scientific dispatching of goods by combining automation with data processing to the highest level in the world today. The central computer system continuously tracks millions of items and bills of lading, while packages are handled and moved automatically. Personnel in the field and the warehouse communicate with computer databases for routing, dispatching, and tracing. It is a real thrill and a revelation to observe how an organization can meld dedicated people and advanced technology into a hectic but harmonious balance. It demonstrates the principle of automation and motivation at its highest. (There's a case study with more about the Federal Express success story on page 208.)

Another Example of Uniqueness That Beat the Competition: Applying Innovation to a Bilge Pump

Innovative thinking requires a special thought discipline. The manager should determine to approach each situation with unconventional rather than conventional wisdom. That requires a different mind-set, but it can be done. Here's an outstanding example involving a decidedly nonglamorous product: a bilge pump.

A small start-up company that had little capital but did have an innovative entrepreneur decided to produce bilge pumps for pleasure boats. Because of a crowded competitive field, innovation was needed. The founder decided to work with standard requirements from a management textbook, but to innovate the implementation of every single element. His thinking went like this:

Standard requirement	Innovation
Market need	Boats need bilge pumps to get rid of water that comes in. Existing pumps often fail because the automatic switches do not actuate or the motors burn out. An innovative design is needed.
Technological innovation	Design an electronic automatic switch with no moving parts, and install heat shields on the motor to prevent burnout if the pump is running dry.
Customer appeal	Until now, all pumps have been a practical black because no one sees them in the bottoms of boats. But customers do see them at the marine store, so use colorful plastic and attractive design for the pump housings.
Advertising	Small companies can't afford a large advertising budget. Solution: Offer a $3000 prize for the speedboat winning a prestigious ocean race while equipped with the new pump. Attach an advertising decal to the bow of all participating boats. The winning boat will be pictured leaping out of the water on the covers of most yachting magazines, providing an extensive free-advertising bonanza.
Customer satisfaction	Copy Sears' powerful motivator from year 1890: "Satisfaction Guaranteed or Your Money Back." Please dealers and customers by accepting exchanges with no paperwork and no questions asked. Make them love us.
Systems approach to customers' needs	Pump buyers don't want pumps—they want water out of their boats. Don't just sell them pumps: instead, provide them with all the items they need to *install* the pumps; through-hull fittings, screws, plastic hoses, stainless-steel clamps, electrical wires, switches, connectors—all neatly packaged and ready. No more multiple trips to the hardware store for items that might or might not be right for the job.
Product line extension	Offer the customer a choice of pumps, because boats come in small, large, and intermediate sizes. Design various sizes of pumps to fit the market needs, but maintain the same shapes and colors for product line identification.
Diversification	Diversification can be profitable, but it should be related to the original business. Recreational vehicles represent a market similar to that of pleasure boats. The difference is that water doesn't need to be pumped out but needs to be pumped in—from water tank to sink. Make the minor design changes that will enable the bilge pump to do this.

Postscript. When a smallie becomes very successful, a biggie gets interested. One has a choice of feeding an elephant or being trampled. In this case, the bilge pump manufacturer sold his thriving business to a larger company. He put half of his gains into a savings account and with the other half started another small, innovative company.

Establishing Uniqueness in Packaging: The Brik Pak Success Story

One way to beat the competition by 10 percent: Repackage old products in innovative new clothes with a touch of added convenience. It's a strategy that boosts sales. Gillette has done well with a brush–shaving cream dispenser. Toothpaste pump dispensers now make up 12 percent of the toothpaste market. Aziza has come up with a nail polish pen, while Liquid Tide has a drip-proof spout and a combination bottle cap–measuring cup.

One outstanding example is the Brik Pak, an airtight container made of paperboard and plastic with aluminum foil in between. It keeps perishables fresh for 5 months *without* refrigeration. The originator, Tetra Pak —a $2.8 billion private Swedish company— converted 40 percent of western Europe milk sales to its aseptic package.

The company introduced the system to the United States in 1977, mostly for juices. At first, results were dismal: Total sales through 1981 were only $3.5 million. Despite this, the U.S. subsidiary (Brik Pak, Inc.) built a $40 million plant and a $10 million research facility. The timing of this risky decision was right. Unit sales in 1984 were 1 billion aseptic containers; soared to 1.7 billion containers in 1986, and continue to climb.

The Brik Pak has several important advantages:

- *Lower direct cost.* A 1-liter box costs 50 percent less than cans, 30 percent less than bottles. Overall cost reduction for bottlers after filling is 18 percent.
- *Lower indirect cost.* No need for refrigerated storage or shipping.

- *Taste advantage.* The aseptic process requires briefer sterilization heating than canning; flavors retain more natural taste.
- *Customer convenience.* An 8-ounce box with a built-in straw becomes the choice for snacks and box lunches, opening new markets with its portability.

The new packaging also has product line extension potential, including the milk, wine, and soft drink markets (but the latter only if the package can be made rigid enough to hold carbonated contents).

However, there is a disadvantage for the innovating company: Success breeds fast and powerful competition. Already U.S. Combibloc—a joint venture of R.J. Reynolds Industries, Inc. and Jagenberg of West Germany—is "cardboarding" Hawaiian Punch. Continental, X-Cello, International Paper, American Can, and others also are coming out with their versions of the Brik Pak.

But Brik Pak represents a classic example of good planning and successful new product innovation. The same steps can be applied to many nonrelated businesses:

1. Find a proven market outside the United States. Other countries have dramatically increased their innovative abilities and are pioneering major breakthroughs before the United States does. Pen dispensers, pump dispensers, and new juice containers were being used in Europe long before sudden U.S. popularity. Imitation is the sincerest form of flattery and lots cheaper. Monitor offshore technological and marketing developments. Don't display a provincial attitude or be reluctant to copy and adapt. Act like the Japanese for a change.
2. Accept (financially and emotionally) a high risk factor. New approaches require a critical mass of venture capital. One must be prepared to spend and invest on nonsure things. Capital can be found through joint ventures, equity offerings, and silent partners—all of which require the sharing of both risk and return.
3. Develop a new product that offers advantages to both the producer and the ultimate user. This is a key factor. Brik Pak, for instance, is a cheaper package for the juice maker and a genuine convenience for the consumer. Look for the double-whammy advantage.

4. Start immediately on product-line extension. A successful product must have the capability to be modified to fit into additional markets.
5. Move strongly and rapidly to offset the inevitable me-too competition.

Potential Winners in the Innovation Sweepstakes

Innovation is flourishing. There are more new products, new processes, and new services than there are resources to exploit them. It's a question of proper selection, often more intuitive than analytical. Here's a sampling of potential winners:

- *Medical identity card.* Nineteen-year-old Douglas Becker developed a plastic identity card capable of displaying not only 500,000 words but also graphs and pictures. Blue Cross and Blue Shield of Maryland pioneered by distributing LifeCards to 1.6 million subscribers. Each LifeCard contains up to 800 pages of individual medical data, including x-rays, EKGs, and prescriptions. Other applications are endless and exciting.
- *Instant beer.* Brasserie du Pecheur, a small brewery in Alsace, claims a process to create instant beer with a beer concentrate to which you simply add water and the desired alcohol level at the point of sale. If the taste is really the same, potential savings in distribution and packaging are immense and exciting.
- *Plastic bottle caps.* Jim Smith, president and major shareholder of H-C Industries, Inc., pioneered a revolution in soft drink bottle closures. Traditional metal crowns and aluminum roll-ons may soon be replaced by billions of H-C Wing-Lok plastic caps. The entrepreneurial spirit of a small company with limited resources has outproduced lethargic giants like Reynolds and Alcoa. The latter acquired H-C in 1986—and made the original stockholders wealthy. (See Case Study Twelve, page 211.)
- *Computers for musicians.* Cardiff University has developed a computerized music-writing device. A computer recognizes any note and writes what it hears. It will help composers bridge the gap between creative inspiration and the tedious process of writ-

ing each note down in the centuries-old way. It will also facilitate accurate tuning of instruments.

- *Intercontinental publishing.* *The Financial Times of London* (one of the best newspapers in the world) has inaugurated a high-technology communications system to provide early distribution in major North American cities. The contents are transmitted from London via Intelsat V satellite to local U.S. printing presses. Perhaps *USA Today* could become *World Today*.
- *Educational videotapes.* Over 27 million U.S. households have videocassette recorders—and the number is growing by 7 million a year. Consumers may buy 14 million special-interest tapes in 1986 vs. 6 million last year. The movie cassette is mostly a one-time rental business, but tapes on cooking, golf, exercising, and self-improvement are purchased for repeated viewing. Prices are as low as $9.95, and the variety is incredible; the *Index to Educational Video Tapes* lists 55,000 titles! Some tapes are discounted because they include advertising (an example is P&G's *American Woman* video magazine with 6 minutes of commercials). The field is still new, and many entrants will fail; but what an opportunity for new ideas and new markets!
- *Fingerprint identification.* Automatic fingerprint reading seemed to be around the corner in 1970, but it was turned into a practical reality only recently. Not by IBM or by any other electronics giant, but by a small, persistent entrepreneur, Michael Schiller. The device has great potential beyond the conventional restricted-access identification. It could be used in airports to guard against terrorists and also, in a more mundane but huge market, to verify the bearer of a credit card or check. Positive, foolproof, and fast identification is a must in today's increasingly cashless society. The present pioneer is Fingermatrix, Inc. of North White Plains, New York, but many others are just a step behind.

To Beat the Competition, You Must Make Innovation a Way of Life

Clue management is the practice of reading between the lines and detecting trends. It means thinking laterally to transform and adapt seemingly unrelated factors into profitable new business propositions. It requires a mind that's curious, dissatisfied, and alert. The Japanese call it *sunao,* the "untrapped mind," which is free from self-centeredness and eagerly receptive to ideas from outside.

We'll talk more about clue management and the technique of razor blade reading, as well as the invaluable technique of pyramid thinking, in Part IV. Here let's discuss how innovation can be stimulated, encouraged, and nurtured. We must make it a way of life in our companies by motivating and rewarding people for their contributions. Triple your present efforts to achieve a *continuous flow* of innovative programs in your organization. This is a must because:

- The faster rate of technological breakthroughs will obsolete your "uniqueness" in a shorter time.
- Technology is no longer a U.S. exclusive: 51 percent of U.S. patent office applications are now foreign, as opposed to 20 percent in the good old days.
- Customers are more fickle, demanding, and pluralistic. They want new things and new ways in shorter intervals.

The future depends on the creativity of the present. Faster rate of change demands that an organization create a substantial number of innovations to keep up with new technologies and fiercer competition. Innovation stems from ideas, many ideas—most of them useless, some good, and a few extraordinary.

Brilliant breakthrough ideas don't usually just happen. The inventions by accident (dynamite, Post-It™ glue, Nutrasweet) are exceptions. Innovation is hard work. A company must deliberately create a culture and policies to encourage the creation, presentation, evaluation, and implementation of ideas.

Greater innovation—in new products and services, marketing, and cost reduction—does not mean tripling budgets. That's the brute force way to disaster. Innovation is achieved by finding, hiring, motivating, and nurturing talented individuals in your company. Do you attract them and keep them?

Personnel at all levels should and can be taught to think creatively. Books and courses abound (Drucker, De Bono, Tucker, Rowan, and many others). The methods are known: derivative thinking, lateral thinking, brainstorming. But it takes a top-executive commitment to give high priority to the process of companywide innovation. Usually, it's just lip service.

Monday Morning Actions

- Review your present programs and processes for generating and evaluating new ideas, suggestions, and innovative proposals.
- Provide facilities for rapid upward communication of ideas.
- Provide prompt and constructive evaluation by qualified personnel with decision-making powers.
- Provide meaningful and immediate rewards for accepted proposals; provide extraordinary rewards for extraordinary ideas.
- Provide rapid implementation of accepted innovations.
- Provide companywide publicity and hoopla on new ideas and new actions.
- Put more management stress on innovation, including tangible encouragement through availability of time, seed money, instruction, databases, and so on.
- Make an inventory of the exceptional and talented people in your organization.
- Institute specific programs to motivate *all* employees to practice innovative thinking such as directed brainstorming sessions.
- Make creativity an important and integral part of the company's culture.
- Test yourself as to the number and quality of new ideas you implemented this year.

Which Strategy to Beat the Competition—Commodity or Specialty?

To beat the competition by 10 percent, you must select appropriate strategies to fit your organization's capabilities. In starting your analysis, you should evaluate two generic strategies: commodity and specialty.

A commodity business produces goods and services that have no differentiation from the competition except possibly price. To prosper in the commodity business, a company must have two key characteristics:

- It must be a low-cost producer worldwide, able to out-price anyone else and make a profit. (That requires high capital investment and the latest technology and facilities.)
- It must have deep pockets to withstand predatory price wars by powerful and often ill-managed competitors.

Unless both criteria can be met, one should not go the commodity route. It's no longer a viable strategy for most companies today, because they lack the resources to withstand extreme fluctuations in raw material costs and predatory price wars by powerful competitors and also lack the ability to out-price anyone and still make a profit.

The second generic strategy is the specialty business. This business possesses a real or perceived uniqueness (other than price) that attracts customers through patents, service, delivery, quality, selection, charisma, or whatever works.

A basic planning task is to evaluate a company's strengths and weaknesses relevant to the two primary strategies.

The Specialty Strategy: Commodity Companies Can *Change Their Spots*

Many commodity businesses are getting away from the commodity game by changing their basic strategies. This is not an instant metamorphosis; it takes dedicated, focused long-term strategy and implementation. Hercules is an example of successful transition. It shifted over a period of 5 years from commodity to specialty petrochemicals and at the same time diversified into unrelated fields to reduce its dependence on the petrochemical market.

Uniroyal and Goodrich are pursuing the same objective: to reduce their dependence on the tire business and eventually even get out of tire manufacturing completely. And a long time ago, Textron divested itself of all its original textile interests.

The obvious mistake in nonrelated diversification is to enter unknown fields without specific management and market knowledge. Instructive examples are Kroger in financial services, Xerox in insurance, Hyatt in airlines, and Merrill Lynch in residential real estate. Sometimes it is better to put all your eggs in one basket and watch that basket very carefully.

Even Biggies Want Niches

A market can be divided into two segments. The first is the big slice, dominated by a few large companies. Examples are cereals, tires, computers, aluminum, soft drinks, autos, and cigarettes. In each of these industries, four to six giants divide 80 to 90 percent of the market. Each company fights for an extra 1 percent of market share, which is worth hundreds of millions.

The remaining small slice is populated by hundreds of small concerns, each fighting for a 90 percent share of its 1 percent specialized niche. While Coke and Pepsi play on the center court for big stakes, K-9 Kola Company successfully markets a soft drink for dogs. The demand is much less, but so is the competition.

Niches have become so popular that even giants are now going after markets they once considered beneath their attention. Suddenly, small has become beautiful for the biggies.

In the past, the two slices of the pie were distinct and separate. The biggies had economic power, but they were regulated and institutionalized. The smallies had no clout, but they had a lot of freedom and entrepreneurial spirit.

Today, some biggies are trying to act like smallies and some smallies are trying to act like biggies (usually with disastrous results). But the basic distinction is still there. It is even reinforced by the ongoing extraordinary merger mania.

Precision Marketing Is One Key to Beating the Competition

Everywhere you look in the business world today you will find segmentation. Proper market identification and segmentation are critical for future success. No longer can marketeers use a shotgun to spread their target and simplify their aim. They now must use a rifle and become precision target shooters.

In retailing, K-Mart is aiming at the lower end with big discounts and minimum service. JCPenney is gambling billions on upgrading its image, service, and quality to go upscale. (But will customers go to Penney to buy Gucci originals?) Sears is still in the middle, not yet sure of its new positioning. It's experimenting, but meanwhile it is losing customers and market share.

There's segmentation in the enormous new financial services field as well. First, there are the national mass merchandisers of stocks, bonds, credit cards, mortgages, insurance, loans, you name it. Because of consolidation, they will be reduced to a dozen or less, including Merrill Lynch, Amex-Shearson-Lehman, Paine Webber, Bache-Prudential, omnipotent Citicorp, and "socks & stocks" Dean Witter–Sears–Coldwell.

Then there will be the discounters, a bargain-basement variety like Schwab, charging low commissions and providing no service. The highly personalized, specialized boutique type will be represented by small regional or local entities geared to the customized, warm "family" feeling, individual attention, and hand holding.

Segmentation and specialization are evident in the fast-food business also. Outlets like McDonald's and Burger King are fighting competition and the slowdown of supergrowth by offering a multichoice menu instead of just hamburgers. Fish, chicken, beef, eggs, and salad, in various combinations and permutations add to the costs, complexity of preparation, and training of employees. The strategy is necessary to preserve market share, but it will probably erode profit margins and increase capital investment. Meanwhile, casualties are mounting among fast-food chains trying to compete with the two biggies. Unless they can offer uniqueness, they're doomed.

It's a similar story with supermarket brands. Because grocery producers are proliferating the types and sizes of their products, there's an intense battle for shrinking shelf space. This makes it likely that only the No. 1 and No. 2 brands will remain in strong positions, because they can invest heavily in R&D, continuous improvement, and huge advertising and promotion campaigns. They will be able to continue to command premium prices.

The other end of the spectrum will be taken by some generics and by a growing volume of private brands. These will be much cheaper, but they will offer reasonable quality. There will be very little, if any, shelf space left for brands No. 3 to No. 6. These middle brands have no uniqueness to offer, and they will find it tough to survive.

But specialties and niche products will thrive: diet foods and gourmet delicacies, microwave convenience foods, ethnic specialties, and so on. It all fits into place: The consumer is emperor.

The Campbell Shift: Different Soups for Different Groups

Even Campbell Soup Company—a commodity producer if there ever was one—is responding to the segmentation of the U.S. consumer market. Campbell has always represented standardization, volume production, and national brand identity. But the cover story of *Business Week*'s January 26, 1987, issue reported:

- Campbell is making its nacho cheese soup spicier for Texas and California than for other parts of the country.
- The company is experimenting with a Creole soup for Southern markets and a red bean soup for Hispanic areas.
- After many years of strictly national advertising, Campbell is regionalizing its marketing efforts to target specific local tastes and fashions.
- With the phenomenal increases in numbers of working women, people living alone, and single-parent households, Campbell's product development efforts are no longer aimed at the traditional family; instead they are aimed at providing the increased convenience, sophistication, and variety that are demanded by today's consumers.

Consumer Whims Must Determine Your Strategy—and Your Opportunities

You can't beat the competition by 10 percent unless you get the jump on your competitors by spotting changing consumer whims early on. Let's talk about some rapidly developing consumer trends that can present tremendous opportunities to alert businesses.

Consumer whims can be compared to love affairs. A classic example: Until a few years ago, U.S. consumers were having deep, long-lasting love affairs with their automobiles. Then, during the 1970s, consumers changed lovers.

For decades, the family car not only meant friendly transportation but represented a symbol of freedom and prosperity. Americans would anxiously wait for the weekend to load the family for a long drive to the country, where they would look for an eating place advertising home cooking.

Then OPEC brought about high gas costs. Inflation-driven car prices, combined with congested roads and scarce parking spaces, soured the love affair. (Also, crime on the streets inhibited going out.) The automobile became just transportation.

That's when American consumers found a new lover: television. We are becoming a stay-at-home society of video addicts. From 4½ hours a day in 1950 we have increased our daily viewing time to over 7 hours. And additional enhancements, such as cable, multiple channels, VCRs, cassette rentals, stereo sound, and home recording, will add even more viewing hours in years to come.

The stay-at-home trend is being reinforced by the growth of catalog shopping, electronic shopping, at-home exercise equipment, and telecommuting (already some 7 million people work out of their homes, and the potential is for 10 million more).

This represents a major change in American lifestyle that creates new markets and generates many business opportunities:

- *Equipment:* Large TV sets, flat TV tubes, better sound systems, recorders, cameras, portables, new screen copiers, modular system components, dish antennas
- *Furniture:* TV-centered living rooms, built-ins, wall units, cabinets
- *Foods and eating habits:* Convenience foods, microwave packaging (to permit meal preparation during commercial breaks), snacks, soft drinks, and a new generation of dietary concoctions

Cashing in on the Communications Revolution

The current love affair with television is not just a passing infatuation. It constitutes an exciting new social era. Breakthroughs in electronic technology made Americans return to their homes after advances in automobile technology lured them away.

But the TV and home entertainment explosion is just one part of an even more important revolution in communications at home and at the office. Fiber optics technology permits sending video, audio, and data through a common transmission medium at efficient, economical rates. Smaller-diameter dish antennas will achieve the same results through commercial satellite operations.

Those developments will create monumental changes in our society and our lifestyles. Any home can be economically linked to many different sources of entertainment, knowledge, business, and communications. People can enhance their lives by:

- Acquiring additional knowledge (superior home education through audio and video)
- Saving much tedious effort (direct banking, paying bills) and shopping time (direct electronic catalog ordering)
- Choosing from an extensive entertainment menu—90 or more channels of movies, theater, music, sports, and interactive games
- Establishing two-way communications—voting, polling, and financial transacting through audio and print

This isn't science fiction; it's a present-day reality within the reach of millions of consumers. The size of the potential market is limited only by imagination. Most enterprises and institutions will be affected in some way.

Now is the time to analyze, evaluate, and set scenarios for the future. Many opportunities exist for smaller companies. The giants will dominate because of the need for large capital investments. But the huge variety of applications, services, and equipment inherent in the multifunction "home communications" market presents many profitable niches for smaller innovators.

Monday Morning Actions

- Ask yourself how the stay-at-home trend affects your business, directly or indirectly.
- Find an opportunity for your business—and act on it.

Getting into the Growing Service Market

The extraordinary growth in services per capita indicates a basic structural change and a radical reallocation of consumer budgets and interests. In response to this trend, companies not already in the service field should refocus their activities and take advantage of growing opportunities in this area; it's a good way to beat your competition by 10 percent. Here are some potentially profitable possibilities:

1. Enter a service sector (e.g., industrial retraining).
2. Add a service element to your products (e.g., barter of high-price copier supplies for yearly maintenance contract).
3. Concentrate on products required to support a growth service (e.g., cable TV expansion and new programming will stimulate sales of TV sets with large screens and stereo capabilities).
4. Sell solutions to customers' problems, not just products.
5. Provide consulting to other firms based on your specialized knowledge.
6. Sell total systems to consumer markets.
7. Rent physical resources (warehousing, computer time) to other companies.
8. Finance customers' purchases of your products.
9. Offer management of your products (installation, maintenance, and operation).
10. Distribute through your own retail chain or outlets.
11. Handle distribution internally; eliminate the middleman.
12. Provide services that are innovative and new (e.g., Federal Express one-day mail).

Opportunities will abound. The service sector is and will continue to be the fastest growing, strongest segment of the U.S. economy. It requires less capital investment than manufacturing, yet it cannot exist without products: movies need projectors; banks need automatic teller machines; barbers need electric clippers; restaurants need kitchens. Manufacturers should consider expanding into the service field as an extension of their products.

Try the systems approach. Although generally used by high-tech companies, it can be applied to most consumer markets as a way of providing total service delivery. Actually, the concept is not new. Sears provides it: telephone order, charge account, home delivery, installation, maintenance contract, reliable guarantee.

Today's customers want complete service. Whether you are selling a water softener (provide salt), built-in furniture (design and install), pizza (deliver piping hot), home computers (provide software support and training), or elevators (offer service and preventive maintenance), consider vertical integration toward the ultimate user. Advantages are many:

- You eliminate or reduce expensive part-time middlemen.
- You maintain valuable direct contact with and get feedback from the user.
- You obtain additional revenue from peripherals (service, parts, supplies).
- You close more and faster replacement sales (control of customer).
- You execute better and smarter individualized niche and subniche marketing. Example: While over-65s represent a large market segment, *ailing*-over-65s are a sizable niche for geriatric medical care and ailing-over-65s *living alone* may provide a specialized subniche for at-home visiting nurse care, as well as peripheral related services and products like food and telephone checks.

Find your own subniches to serve ultimate users directly by offering them a complete service approach.

Overlooked Opportunities in the Underground Economy

Deep economic cycles create a roller coaster effect. Severe recessions (1982) are followed by super booms (1984). But even in bad times, the U.S. economy somehow manages to remain quite strong and to provide a high level of standard of living to many more people than are officially recorded. The reason is the big underground economy.

The underground segment of compensation without taxation is the fastest growing part of the U.S. and other industrial economies. Some 15 percent of our GNP—$400 billion to $600 billion—is exchanged without being reported to the IRS. The result is a huge, yearly $100 to $140 billion uncollected federal tax loss, a big part of the entire federal deficit!

This isn't the forum to discuss the reluctance of our elected and appointed officials to enforce the law vigorously. It is, however, a clue to some potential market opportunities. Consider:

- Cheaters (unreported capital gains)
- Criminals (laundered funds)
- Skimmers (owners rifling their own cash registers)
- Moonlighters (e.g., 90 percent of private-duty nurses with unreported income)
- Spongers (undeclared tips)
- Discounters (cheaper if paid in cash)

They all add up to millions of consumers who have more disposable income than is reported through census statistics, employment levels, official income brackets, and other data. Various studies indicate that unreported income is spent not on necessities, but on luxuries and self-indulgence. Thus, many products and services actually may have a greater sales potential and a different category of customers than are shown by conventional market research.

High-priced luxury and specialty producers should review their marketing strategies. This applies to cars, boats, furniture, jewelry, second homes, travel, art objects, and so on. Many markets and niches are being underestimated because untaxed income is not taken into consideration.

Opportunities in Changing Food and Drink Markets

Americans are altering their eating and drinking habits at a fast pace—and creating tremendous opportunities for companies that want to get the jump on their competition. Greater attention to diet and health is combined with an enthusiasm for experimenting with exotic foods. Retail sales of soy foods (tofu, soy sauce for stir frying) climbed from $41 million in 1979 to an estimated $280 million in 1986.

Consumers seek products rich in protein and low in fat and cholesterol. Hard liquor consumption has declined. Chic white wine is off; low-alcohol wine coolers are up. We each drink 163 gallons a year of nonalcoholic beverages—a new record—and soft drink consumption has topped the consumption of tap water for the first time in history.

The trend is up for more natural juice content and for diet "no" drinks (no calories, no caffeine, no additives). In the exotic areas, watch for amaranth (high-protein grain), quinoa (wild rice substitute), and pepino (looks like a tomato, tastes like a strawberry-melon). These are being developed through genetic manipulation.

High consumer awareness and education about health will greatly accelerate major changes in food and drink selection and consumption. Biotechnology will contribute to new types of food (frostproof, high-protein, supercow, etc.).

Advice: Anybody engaged in the food and drink business—grower, processor, manufacturer, packager, distributor, retailer, restaurateur—should take an extra serious look at the new consumer habits and the new prospects of supply and production. The overall food market grows at the 0.9 percent rate of population growth, but a +30 percent trend in one segment will create −30 percent growth in another.

Early clue detection is imperative. Entrepreneurial companies could profit by entering exotic new niches considered too small by the biggies.

Opportunities in Mail-Order Shopping

Mail-order catalog shopping is getting the stamp of approval from U.S. consumers in a big way. Over 6500 catalogs offer everything from exercise equipment and diamonds to lasers and bridles. The industry grew from $36 billion in 1980 to more than $50 billion in 1986, and it keeps steaming ahead. It has big established names like Sears and JCPenney, retailers like Saks, Neiman-Marcus, and Bloomingdale's (mail-order is its second biggest "store"), specialists like L.L. Bean, Land's End, and Goldberg's Marine, and thousands of other niche mail-order marketers.

There are specialty catalogs for meats, Harley-Davidson motorcycle accessories, rare tools, pig memorabilia, you name it. Entrepreneurs are having a field day. Cabela's fishing and hunting gear catalog started in 1961 with $1000; sales topped $100 million by 1984. Chef's Catalog, offering kitchen products, was mailed to 100,000 households in 1977; present volume is 10 million catalogs and $15 million in sales.

Caution: A successful niche in mail-order needs continuous attention and innovation. The flood of catalogs may create a 20 percent casualty rate. The survivors are the ones who will be:

- *Flexible.* Change products and market segments according to demand and response.
- *Reputable.* Refund or exchange merchandise promptly.
- *Cost-conscious.* Automate order filling, packaging, and mailing to offset higher postal rates.
- *Consumer-conscious.* Retain a feel for the market; keep in *personal* touch.

Superdiscounting: A Growing Market

The traditional homogeneous U.S. middle class is splitting into two distinct classes: high and low earners. In 5 years, goods-producing employment lost 1 million workers while the service-producing sector gained 8 million. This created a significant shift in buying power. Service workers, who now constitute 74 percent of the total work force, earn 25 to 45 percent less than manufacturing and construction workers. Of the 8 million jobs created since 1981, according to the Congressional Joint Economic Committee, nearly three-fifths paid less than $7000 a year. The low-earner group keeps growing as services displace industrial production.

There's an opportunity in this phenomenon. Low earners seek low prices. Superdiscounting attracts buyers to 100,000 square foot frill-free warehouses. These stores have limited assortments—5000 items vs. 50,000 in large discount stores. But they feature top-brand, first-quality merchandise.

Warehouse Clubs, mixtures of wholesale and retail membership operations, grew in 8 years to a $2 billion volume. Over 100 outlets had $4 billion in sales by the end of 1985, and analysts forecast 350 warehouses grossing $20 billion by 1990.

Several retailers are making good profits by targeting low-income shoppers. Dollar General Stores specialize in items mostly under $10 sold in 6000 square foot stores, with only three employees, located in rural and inner-city areas. Although the market is big—36 percent of all households earn less than $15,000—there are relatively few competitors because traditional discounters are upgrading their wares, their stores, and their locations.

The low-end niche is served by merchandisers that know their customers' lifestyles and understand their customers' behaviors. Poor people have to buy cheap goods and only when they really need them. This opens an opportunity for low-cost distribution, bottom-dollar imports, irregulars, and second-hand goods.

Advice to Retailers: Explore innovative ways of profitably attracting a growing segment of lower-income buyers through major discounting, 30 to 40 percent below regular discount retail prices.

Selling the Singles: Another 10 Percent Opportunity

Over 21 million Americans (12 percent of the adult population) are living alone. They're hot prospects for niche goods and services.

The singles category is composed of diverse groups with different characteristics:

- Baby-boomers in the 25 to 29 age bracket are 39 percent single men and 26 percent single women.
- Of all singles, 60 percent are women (30 percent widows), 50 percent are middle income, but 44 percent earn under $10,000 a year.
- The number of elderly women will grow at twice the population rate and live 20 years longer vs. 16 years longer for men.

Recommendations: Target specific singles for specific services. "Permanent" upper-class singles buy big houses and stylish furniture, travel a lot, and purchase luxury items. Food makers should target working singles for gourmet frozen meals and prepackaged salad bars. Senior singles over 65 will need special dietary and enriched food preparations.

Car companies should court the female buyer (42 percent of purchases) who often is single. So are 54 percent of condominium purchasers. By 1995, some 27 million singles will be expecting products and services that are purposely designed for them. Fascinating market!

Beating the Competition on Quality Is a Must

No matter what strategic directions a business takes in its product development and marketing, the management thinking key word should be *quality*. Quality of products, quality of service, quality of personnel, quality of management, quality of profits. That last—quality of profits—is a fundamental that needs very thoughtful attention because it requires balancing the present and the future, with an emphasis on the future.

Don't compete on price. Unless you are really the lowest-cost producer and have deep pockets (to withstand losses while the price war destroys your competition), price competition will erode and destroy your business.

Nor should you try to beat the competition by reducing margins, which is simply a rationalization of a price reduction. Instead, work on cost reduction, subcontracting, modernizing, reducing break-even points, innovating. Figure out how to *increase* margins by expanding support of the product line through repairs, preventive maintenance, supplies, planned replacement, leasing, operating, training. A philosophy of positive, constructive, creative solutions must replace the sales department's cries of "We must cut prices!"

Competitive war should be based on value, not on price. True or perceived value must be marketed, provided, and believed by customers. The extra value may reside in quality, service, delivery, integrity, responsiveness, financing, or whatever the customer perceives as equivalent to a price differential. This concept of value must be worked on constantly and consistently.

Right Now, U.S. Products Are Losing the Quality War

The label "Made in U.S.A." once represented an assurance of quality and reliability. For many people in recent years, it has become a warning. As incidents of shoddy workmanship and defective operation of U.S. goods abound, consumers and industrial purchasers turn to new sources abroad. Even with the weakened dollar, this has continued to be true. Quality is often the primary reason for preferring imports.

In a business section article on December 14, 1986, *The New York Times* painted this picture of the import phenomenon:

> It is a pattern that cuts across income and educational levels, that defies political ideology and national pride. Wealthy Americans want the cachet of the German Mercedes, while the budget-conscious gravitate toward a Korean Hyundai. The people who sound like the most avid proponents of "buy American" will buy Japanese appliances, Italian shoes, and Taiwanese sports clothes.... All told, the United States is the premier export market for 15 countries. The volume of imports has increased by 80 percent in the past four years, more than twice the rate of growth in previous, albeit shorter, economic expansions, according to Stephen S. Roach, senior economist for Morgan Stanley & Company.
>
> Washington policy makers have tried to reverse the trend by driving down the dollar. But the effort so far has made but a small dent in America's huge import appetite. Foreign producers apparently have the allegiance of many American customers, regardless of slight price increases.

No categories of products seem to be exempt, not even computers and machine tools, both traditional U.S. domains. Japanese and other imported cars are not cheaper, yet they took 30 percent of the U.S. market in 1986 versus 6 percent in 1965.

Why? They're better made, despite the multimillion dollar advertising claims by U.S. car makers. A survey by the American Society for Quality Control concludes that 75 percent of the public thinks foreign-made products are equal to or better than domestic goods.

Many industrial buyers—who are more objective and less prone to emotionalism—agree. Over 600 Grumman Flxible buses were taken off New York City's streets because of dangerous flaws. Rockwell International subway cars cost the company over $70 million in damages. Italian and Japanese mass transit systems cost 10 to 20 percent less and have no start-up troubles.

H.J. Heinz purchased German-made labeling machinery because of lower maintenance, higher reliability, faster production, and more precise labeling than were provided by U.S. equivalents. Coors Brewing also uses foreign labeling equipment, as well as British-made racking for kegs. TV stations increasingly switch to $50,000 Sony minicams.

These are not isolated examples. They add mightily to the $140 billion—and growing—U.S. trade deficit.

Responding to this trend are a growing movement and determination to restore the quality image and performance within many U.S. companies. Top executives are being appointed to be in sole charge of quality control. It has taken a large loss in market share to shake a large number of enterprises out of their costly complacency.

The drive for higher quality is a result of several new factors. First, the consumer is better educated, smarter, more discriminating, and more demanding. Consumers can no longer be intimidated by the store or supplier. They have multiple choices and many ways to get exactly the merchandise or service they really want.

Second, advances in technology make product quality and reliability normal, expected conditions. These attributes no longer command a premium price.

Managers must decide on the key criteria for the future successes of their businesses—and providing high-quality goods and services is probably the most important strategy to start implementing at once.

It is often incomprehensible why companies fail to act on this "platitude." Yet Commodore's hot-selling home computer had return rates of 20 to 30 percent from dealers because of defects. Control Data stopped production of its trouble-plagued disk drive and took big write-offs that contributed to an overall quarterly loss. Not even IBM is exempt from quality surprises from its suppliers, as shown by its serious problems with disk drives on its AT personal computer.

Many companies put major pressure on their subcontractors, often placing their own inspection personnel on a supplier's premises. But inspection is not the answer. The goods should be fault-free on the first run.

Automation and motivation are better answers than inspection. Canon is a superb example of this. Its main camera plant north of Tokyo is superautomated by robots and the latest electronically programmed and controlled equipment. Still, 2000 employees are needed, mostly for the complex final assembly. They are trained to avoid "nine wastes," including defects of any kind.

Somebody must have done it right: Out of 470,000 units produced in 3 months, only 2 were defective.

Japanese Quality Is Better—So Let's Learn from the Japanese

Japan's prestigious annual award for the highest-quality producer is the Deming medal. It is a way to honor not only outstanding Japanese enterprises, but also to pay tribute to Dr. W. Edwards Deming. Ironically, it was this American who, in 1950, started the quality revolution in Japan.

He was invited that year by the Union of Japanese Scientists and Engineers (JUSE) to speak on statistical quality-control methods. He remained in Japan, and his influence became extraordinary. It still is, almost 40 years later.

Deming was also finally recognized, in a way, in his own country: A large car maker hired the retired scientist to consult on quality-control improvement.

Another American has been honored in Japan: Lawrence D. Miles. Hitachi, Matsushita, and Fujita corporations were given the first Miles Award for their work in value analysis. Miles devised the value analysis system in 1940, and it was enthusiastically adopted by large Japanese companies after the war. Hitachi alone has over 250 value analysis engineers. It credits the value analysis system for savings of over $430 million a year.

Among the key factors contributing to Japanese worldwide success, high consistent quality rates on top. It's more than a strategy; it's a fanatical dedication that pays off handsomely.

Automation and motivation were discussed previously. The Japanese recognize that they go together; people will always be needed to monitor the machines. These people must be both knowledgeable and motivated if high quality is to be maintained.

Japanese companies also set lower short-term financial objectives than do U.S. companies. This does not mean that the Japanese operate on low margins; it means that they plow back into their businesses much higher percentages of earnings than U.S. corporations do. They are more future-minded, and they invest more toward their long-term goals. They put their money where their mouths are. Japanese managers are always striving to learn more about management, the latest techniques, and different methods.

All of those factors have become integral parts of Japan's culture. The company is also the family, and it must be given equal dedication of one's time and efforts. It is not as alien as it sounds: Many employees of IBM, Delta, Johnson & Johnson, Hewlett-Packard, Lincoln Electric, and other U.S. companies with a Japanese mentality feel the same way.

Higher Japanese quality can also be attributed to a basic difference between the Japanese and the U.S. decision-making process. A top-management decision in a U.S. company is made—after due thought, analysis, and input—in the executive suite and is then announced to the organization. And nothing happens. That is because lower echelons do not understand, do not like, or do not know how to implement the edict from above. They have to be sold, instructed, and trained before the decision can be implemented.

The Japanese also make the important decision at the top, but they don't announce it. Instead, they sell, discuss, and dissect the proposed action with everyone who will be directly or indirectly involved in it. That takes time and patience and appears to move at a snail's pace. But it also provides feedback and ideas that may modify the decision. Since it has not yet been announced, it can be changed without loss of face.

But when the decision *is* finally announced, all the key pieces are in place and action starts immediately. The Japanese semiconsensus method brings action 30 percent faster than the U.S. decision process. Many U.S. companies have recognized this, and they are testing the Japanese method.

Recommendations: The word and actions must come from the top: The CEO must establish credibility that the company will be driven by quality and service at all levels of operations. Larger companies may appoint a VP of quality to report directly to the CEO and to have dictatorial powers to enforce the quality commitment. But beware: The first time you still knowingly ship "slightly substandard" goods to the customer, because of tight deadlines or other pressures, your credibility at the grass roots is gone. "They really don't mean it upstairs; they're just talking." Which is your culture?

We Have a Service Economy without Service—and That Presents a Tremendous Opportunity for Beating the Competition by 10 Percent

The overall level of personal service is deteriorating in the United States and throughout the world:

- Store clerks are uninformed, disinterested, and rude.
- Bank tellers are slow and unable to handle the slightest exception to routine.
- Waiters are neither gracious nor attentive—and are often invisible.
- Auto salesmen abandon the buyer the moment the order is signed.
- Taxi drivers take their passengers for a ride.
- Hotel registration and checkout staff challenge room service staff to the "How slow can we be?" game (even in Switzerland).
- Deliveries are late; promises are broken; appointments are not kept; repairs are faulty; orders are incomplete.

United States consumers have been acclimated and conditioned to substandard treatment—they expect it. This presents a tremendous opportunity to any business that provides a service. You can exploit expectations of bad service by applying the Kami *double-negative-whammy strategy.*

It's deceptively simple: Provide a level of service measurably, but not extraordinarily, better than the competition's. The customer will perceive this to be superlative performance, and the degree of satisfaction and the volume of repeat business will be utterly amazing.

What does it cost to answer phones by the fourth ring, call back about a delay, smile, pay attention to customer questions, offer unsolicited help, return phone calls promptly, check after service for feedback, send additional information, explain what the customer wants to know? Not much, but the return on investment is tremendous.

Since few service organizations operate that way (Federal Express and United Parcel are two of the exceptions), a large market also is open for automation of services: automatic teller machines; self-service equipment for stores, restaurants, and gas stations; self-check-in at airports; vending machines, dispensers, and—who knows—perhaps even automatic haircut booths.

If Only More Service Were Like This!

Even though customer service is generally deteriorating, there are notable exceptions that make you feel good. When a complex electrical switch failed on my boat in Florida, I called American Solenoid Company in New Jersey, the distributors of cam-operating rotary switches and relays made by Kraus & Naimer of Austria. Their immediate help to a small, indirect customer was unbelievable. They contacted Ray Parello, a regional vice president who happened to be in Florida. On his way to dinner with his mother, he stopped at my dock, took off his coat and tie, crawled into a cramped compartment, and found that the fault was with the installation, not the switch. Nevertheless, he worked for 2 hours and completely solved the problem.

Obviously, I won't forget him or American Solenoid.

On the other hand, my wife and I stayed at the Helmsley Palace in New York, assured by Mrs. Helmsley's magazine ads of superior personal service. What we experienced instead was a rude bellman, an uncooperative concierge, undelivered messages, long waits for telephone operators, and no hot water. Also no apology. It's easy to advertise, more difficult to deliver.

Market Research, Yes—but Better and Faster

Precision, rifle-shot marketing is an absolute must for successful operation of any business today. Successful companies gather very thorough, detailed information not only about their present and potential customers but about their indirect customers—the ultimate consumers—as well. Today's era of increased pluralism, segmentation, and subcultures requires complete dedication to customer orientation.

Advances in computers (cheaper memories with faster access) make comprehensive customer databases economically feasible. Complete histories, ordering patterns, likes and dislikes, and even personalities of individual customers or classes of customers should be available, properly updated, and carefully evaluated.

Although this recommendation seems obvious, many enterprises still lack an adequate, automated customer database. Many of them object to the cost of continuous research, upgrading, and analysis programs. They claim great difficulty in acquiring detailed information about their customers. My recommendation is to spare neither money nor effort to procure and maintain a sophisticated customer database for each of your markets, products, and services. Thoughtful use of the information by all departments (not just marketing) will repay the effort many times over.

Market research must not only be better—it must be done faster and acted upon faster. When you have a winner, the imitators are in the market within months, not within years as in the good old days. Thus, there is no time for paralysis through analysis and a corporate "let's wait and see" attitude. The emphasis is on fast action, risk taking, entrepreneurship, and innovation.

Recommendations:

- Clear your mind of past experiences.
- Understand your new customers.
- Establish in-depth market research.
- Segment the market into discrete niches with specific characteristics.

- Pursue market and customer analysis on a continuous basis.
- Hire the most knowledgeable marketing professionals that incentives can attract.
- Double the speed of your market analysis.
- Cut your traditional new-product introduction schedule in half.

Can You Beat the Competition by Getting into the Merger Game?

Recent combines in oil, food, chemicals, steel, retailing, financial services, and even accounting don't make much economic sense or provide any new opportunities for additional growth of the partners. Not a single job will be created; many jobs will be lost. In most cases, mergers aren't the way to beat the competition by 10 percent.

Obviously, the goal of every merger is to create synergy, make 2 and 2 equal 5. But in 80 percent of mergers, 2 and 2 have added up to 3. For every good, synergistic, intelligent merger (Dun & Bradstreet and Nielsen), there are four bad, inane, destructive ones (Fluor and St. Joe Minerals, Sohio and Kennecott, Mobil and Montgomery Ward, U.S. Steel and Marathon Oil).

Simultaneously, the same companies claim they're trying to promote small-company atmospheres, establish more horizontal organizations, reduce the levels of reporting and supervision, create atmospheres of innovation and creativity, advance entrepreneurship, and motivate employees to higher productivity through self-actualization.

Who are they kidding? Because of the inertia and hardening arteries of large enterprises, it's the smaller, flexible companies that have great opportunities for fast penetration of niches and exploitation of changing conditions. Mergers among smallies could provide a bigger critical mass of resources and facilities without getting entangled in bureaucratic red tape.

What positive factors ensure a successful merger? Here are six big ones:

1. Merge from strength, not weakness. Mergers should enhance, not repair. Repairs must be done internally; there is no instant cure for management problems.
2. The merger should enhance present business. It should reinforce or complement key activities such as marketing (provide new territories), products (create a more complete line), and service (add repair ability).
3. Provide vertical integration toward the customer (not raw materials) such as retail outlets, distribution channels, warehouse facilities.
4. The merging partner should be healthy. Buying a sick company—even at a bargain price—is a mistake. The turnaround takes too much management time and affects the healthy partner.
5. Make provisions to keep good management. It's more difficult than you might expect. Prior owners and entrepreneurs get rich and leave; bureaucrats take over and ruin the acquired company.
6. There should be no significant dilution of stock because of the merger. Overpaying for a company on the basis of future earnings increases expected from synergy is an illusion.

By these tough criteria, 80 percent of recent mergers would never have happened. That's fine, because they were bummers in the first place.

A Much Better Idea: Joint Ventures

Despite merger mania, there is a better, simpler, faster way to forge alliances, reach new objectives, and beat your competition. *Joint ventures* can accomplish everything that mergers can—while avoiding megabuck stock premiums, dilution, heavy debt, digestion pains, culture-change trauma, and accounting surprises. It's a highly recommended concept.

Giants are forming joint ventures: IBM, Sears, and CBS vs. AT&T, Time, Bank of America, and Chemical Bank in two-way home information services; DuPont and N.V. Philips in optical disks; GM with Toyota, Isuzu, Suzuki, and Daewoo vs. Chrysler and Mitsubishi vs. Ford and Fiat in automobiles.

Small private companies that want to preserve their independence also are joining together to pool resources, exchange complementary strengths, and achieve instant critical mass. Small independent advertising agencies formed a cooperative network to serve larger multilocation customers on a worldwide basis, with local-conditions expertise. A printer, a stationer, and a database maintenance computer bureau can together offer a series of innovative services they could not perform alone.

Another combination is the alliance of small firms with big business. Many biggies help small entrepreneurs with advice, physical resources, technical assistance, market access, and venture capital instead of outright purchase. These small companies want to preserve their independence and innovative drive. Tiny American Robot Corporation in Pittsburgh has prestigious partners: Ford, Koppers, and BMW (Germany), but they don't try to control it.

Cooperative R&D should also be seriously considered. After the Japanese manufacturers launched, in 1981, a joint task force to develop artificial intelligence computers (Fifth Generation Computer System Project), 13 U.S. companies banded together in 1983 to create MCC (Microelectronics and Computer Technology Corporation) with the tacit blessing of the Justice Department Antitrust Division. It didn't work because these particular companies didn't try hard enough to make it work. But this doesn't mean that coop R&D won't work.

Opponents of joint R&D cite the danger of collusion, monopoly, or even "burial" of breakthroughs to prevent early obsolescence of existing products. Proponents stress the advantages of joint R&D:

1. Lower costs (elimination of parallel efforts and duplication)
2. Faster results (bigger critical mass of effort)
3. Effective U.S. competition against foreign developments (Japan's consortia organized by MITI and Europe's ESPRIT with a multimillion dollar budget funded by European Community governments and private entities)
4. Better pool of talent (attracted by a stimulating environment)

The key requirement for successful joint ventures: *Genuine partnership based on mutual trust and respect.* Difficult, yes, but very rewarding. Joint ventures concocted by lawyers and decisions based on votes according to ownership formulas will fail, cost time and money, and create bitter resentment in both camps. If a company can't manage a joint venture successfully, it probably couldn't consummate a successful merger either.

The advantages of joint ventures are numerous, but watch for the pitfalls. Many joint ventures fail miserably because the principals can't agree on common goals, policies, programs, actions, or costs. The reason is usually attitude, which must be that of cooperation, equality, and commonality of interest. It should not matter who has the legal majority to swing a vote. You should get rid of the lawyers after they produce their 10 pounds of small print, and managers must act as equal partners, as one dedicated team.

Also, many joint ventures fail because of external factors. A dog food may have all the right ingredients—best vitamin mix, efficient production, and fine distribution—but if the dogs don't like it, curtains!

Here's a noncanine example: videodiscs. The supercombines for the videodisc were impressive and vertically integrated in a clever way. RCA and others lined up an impressive array of partners from product development (movie and TV studios) to production (U.S. and Japanese electronics manufacturers) to retail distribution (major department stores). Unfortunately for all these efforts, consumers did not want the videodisc—they opted for the VCR and videocassette rentals instead. A beautiful theory killed by a brutal gang of facts.

Monday Morning Actions

- Prepare a joint-venture planning matrix so you can explore joint-venture possibilities. List potential partners under geographical markets, distribution, service, warehousing, manufacturing, development, etc.
- Examine the fit.
- Analyze pluses and minuses.
- Make a phone call.

Stripping Down to Bare Essentials Is Another Way to Beat the Competition

Traditional mines-to-markets vertical integration is out. Large companies are weeding out less-profitable operations and subcontracting more and more manufacturing and assembly processes. Automakers purchase more than half of their car components—and sometimes entire cars. Firestone sells a competitor's radial truck tires; GE has stopped making microwave ovens, CAT scanners, and ice makers.

No U.S. consumer electronics company makes VCRs, but all have their labels on Pacific Rim–made products. IBM purchases over 95 percent of its PC parts, mostly from abroad.

It's a new philosophy: Concentrate on whatever is absolutely essential to the business—its uniqueness—and do it in-house (rare technology, delicate channel of distribution, critical manufacturing part, or difficult time element). Subcontract the rest globally to whomever can provide the service most efficiently.

The concept of 100 percent control (managing one's own people and operations) has given way to coordinative control (managing others' people and operations). Proponents call it selective disaggregation and cost-effectiveness; opponents label it disintegration and a danger to U.S. enterprises and our entire economic system.

Basically, however, it's adaptation to reality. The explosion of global knowledge requires faster reaction to technological breakthroughs, changing markets, and worldwide cost-competitiveness. To achieve faster reaction, a business must be flexible. Giant, vertically integrated empires are not flexible; they must change their basic structures to continue to exist. Politics, unions, societal needs, personnel relations, sentiments, and even patriotism have little bearing when the basic problem is survival.

Divestitures of operations are less publicized than takeovers and leveraged buy-outs, but they are, in fact, growing enormously: some 900 in 1984 with a market value of $30 billion.

Selling, of course, requires a buyer. When the unessential operations are too unprofitable to interest even the "ultimate fool" buyer, they must be discontinued. This is called restructuring. In 1985, Union Carbide unveiled its restructuring plan to result in a charge of $900 million and create a loss for the year. It included plant closings and dismissal of 15 percent of the company's white-collar workers.

DuPont is shrinking more quietly; it has closed some twenty businesses over the past few years. Steel industry closings and write-offs add up to billions of dollars. Other write-offs have been:

- Mobil announced the demise of Montgomery Ward's 113-year-old billion dollar catalog business after 5 years of continuous losses.
- High-tech Texas Instruments closed two more plants and laid off 2200 more workers.
- United Technologies closed its Mostek division after investing $945 million in its purchase and operations. It lost $328 million in 10 months of 1985. In 1980, Mostek made $70 million on $360 million in sales; it was the biggest, most profitable chip maker in the world.

Monday Morning Actions

For big companies

- Prepare a realistic action plan for trimming, cutting, and amputating if necessary.
- Schedule the plan for early completion.
- Replace internal vertical integration with global out-sourcing. Don't wait for a crisis.
- Sell entire businesses that no longer fit (or never fitted) into the mainstream of your golden geese—earlier and faster.

For small companies

- Offer reliable, cost-efficient, and flexible subcontracting services to biggies. They will listen with open minds and at high levels.
- Scout for opportunities to buy small operating divisions. Make offers even if the businesses are not ostensibly for sale. You may be pleasantly surprised.

To Be a Winner: Run Smart and Lean

In this era of unpredictable change, the key word for a business manager must be *flexibility*. Fluctuations in world economies, world markets, and world finances will be more extreme and occur more frequently. That means business enterprises must be mentally and structurally geared to faster, more innovative responses. To be winners, top management and the entire organization must learn to turn on a dime.

Recommendations: Market aggressively; spend on promotion and sales; penetrate niches. But...try to do it without expanding facilities, adding personnel, or making long-term commitments. Emphasize subcontracting, fast turnaround, and economic reversibility of decisions. Don't allocate resources—reallocate resources. Run smart and lean—very lean! Reposition your organization by following the basic winning strategies:

15 Basic Winning Strategies

1. Operate with an absolute minimum of personnel.
2. Expand through subcontracting as needs arise.
3. Achieve a significantly lower break-even through automation, horizontal organization, motivation, and computerization.
4. Concentrate on niche marketing.
5. Adopt value pricing (not price competition).
6. Earn a solid reputation for superior quality and exceptional service.
7. Promote companywide innovation through R&D, new ideas, creative personnel, clue management, high rewards, and other motivation.
8. Seek joint ventures for rapid market and product penetration and instant critical mass efforts.
9. Continuously prune lemons from products, services, and markets (fast in, fast out).

10. Invest in the latest techniques: equipment, computers, methods, and market research.
11. Practice zero-inventory techniques.
12. Expand into complementary services.
13. Give your key employees *significant* ownership in the enterprise.
14. Fight and reduce bureaucracy, red tape, nit-picking routines, nonessential operations and procedures.
15. Instill and practice real values: ethics, quality, respect for the individual, fairness to customers, keeping promises. Make sure these values are shared, believed, and implemented by all employees.

TRIGGER POINT EIGHT

Make decisions three times faster, implement them faster—and make sure they are economically reversible.

"Even if you're on the right track, you'll get run over if you just sit there."
Author Unknown

In 1986, a large food corporation bought a small company that was making frozen fruit popsicles and distributing them regionally. As this product was growing in popularity, the giant's strategy was to roll out its brand nationally. But it took its time about doing that. And by the time the giant made the decision, it was too late—because half a dozen other companies had already done it and there was no room left in supermarket freezers for the biggie's brand.

Here's a prime example of why companies today must make decisions faster—3 times faster than they're doing now. And, just as important, these decisions must be *implemented* 3 times faster.

Why? Because the economic life of a decision today is 3 times shorter than in the past—as a result of faster obsolescence, changing technology, and changing consumer desires and needs. There's no use coming up with something 3 years from now or studying something for 4 years before moving on it; by the time you come out with it, it's too late.

In addition to faster decisions and faster implementation, the third important element is reversibility. Unless a major decision is reversible at a sustainable cost, the results of a decision that goes wrong could be catastrophic. And a bad decision must be reversed quickly—management must be ready to turn on a dime when a decision turns out to be a lemon.

First Requirement for Faster Decisions: Better Data

For making decisions 3 times faster, you need better data from both the external environment and your internal environment.

From the external environment you need better data on the ultimate consumer, not just your direct customer. You must be able to spot changing consumer trends and respond fast.

You may say, "But I make gears—why do I have to know what the consumer wants? The consumer doesn't buy gears." Perhaps so, but as we pointed out in a previous chapter, the ultimate consumer is emperor. Your gears may go into canning machines, and those canning machines may be purchased by Campbell Soup. Your ultimate customers are in supermarkets buying soup.

What if they decide they prefer Brik Pak plastic containers to cans? And Campbell Soup responds to consumer pressure by putting all its soups into Brik Pak containers? If you happen to be a manufacturer of canning machine gears, you'll go broke—unless you had the foresight to scan the external environment and detect the ultimate consumer demand that could affect your product.

To respond to fast-developing changes, you need not just periodic data; you need a *continuous* input—nonstop. Example: If you're in the supermarket business, you can't afford to take inventory just once a month. You must do it perpetually. You must know, day by day, hour by hour, night by night, what people are buying. If you have 200 products vying for a shelf that will take 20 products, you want to know which 20 products people are going to buy.

The information revolution has made data widely and rapidly available. Statistical, economic, market, consumer, and technical data are available in machine-readable form in increasing scope and variety. Commercial and governmental databases provide any type of cross-reference about the external environment—and the access time has become instantaneous. The problem is selection, not availability. Ease of manipulating data offers possibilities for analysis never before available. Again the problem is that of selection. What is the best cut or perspective for "massaging" the abundance of data for best results?

All of this leads to a single recommendation: The manager must be psychologically attuned to this brave new world and must also be technically knowledgeable about the multiple sources of pertinent information, the means and costs of access, and the best ways to transform this raw material into useful data. Understanding information management and selecting data that lead to best actions are new, complex, time-consuming activities. But they must become key ingredients of executive talent. To delegate these new fields of expertise would be to indirectly abdicate the primary executive decision-making function.

The chief executive officer—or at least the division head—must lead in changing management philosophy and adapting the style best suited to the age of information. The common objection to establishing a network of terminals is cost, but the real objection is that executives must, reluctantly, change personal managerial habits. The executive station system requires a manager to learn to work with a terminal, use a keyboard, understand basic computer rules, form a conversation mode with an inanimate object, and become highly knowedgeable about the type and availability of data in the business. It further requires a complex but essential process of setting up central shared databases. This means that the manager must study, analyze, and specifically decide what data are necessary to run the business and in what form. This, obviously, should be done even without automation, but it seldom is.

Too Much Information?

There is a drawback to having access to the vast amounts of data and information that computer technology can provide. As business writer Elizabeth M. Fowler pointed out on February 24, 1987, in *The New York Times,* corporations can become buried under tons of printouts. In the article, John Diebold of the Diebold Group Inc., a management consulting concern, is quoted as saying that this is becoming "a massive problem." Technically trained specialists in management information systems "either perpetuate the past or guess what should be retrieved." Diebold recommends that those in charge should know what information is meaningful and can help a company increase productivity, cut costs, and develop products or services. One solution, he believes, is to have managers who are trained both in broad managerial responsibilities and in specialized management information system skills. The University of Pittsburgh's Graduate School of Business already offers a program that will give students an MBA plus a master of science degree in the management of management information systems.

Since faster decisions are built on fast access to the right information, this may be the time to appoint a top executive responsible for assuring optimum information availability in every phase of business operations. As terminals and end-user activities proliferate, information processing is no longer limited to the MIS department. A chief information officer (CIO) should help channel data to wherever it's needed. It must be done with companywide perspective, organization understanding, and a genuine desire to serve the users. It is not a job for a bureaucrat or nitpicker. It requires continuously updated technical knowledge combined with a keen, practical business sense. The CIO should coordinate the best means of acquiring, storing, processing, retrieving, and distributing all types of information and data: alphanumeric, text, image, and voice.

Second Requirement for Faster Decisions: Better Communication

Just having databases is not sufficient for making faster decisions and implementing them. Shared access to these databases is all-important. This sounds like a technological problem, but actually it's a psychological one.

The problem arises because managers *don't want to share information.* Marketing won't share data with production, which won't share data with financial. The attitude is: This is secret; this information belongs to our department.

It's understandable that middle managers fear sharing information and are resisting shared databases the most fiercely. There's a basic reason: Middle managers are really messengers. They move information up and down. If someone can get information by simply tapping into a shared database, middle managers have lost their function. That's why, when Exxon let go of 40,000 employees and AT&T let go of 25,000, most of them were middle managers.

It's an unfortunate situation, but businesses must face reality. To be competitive today, the speed of decision making must be tripled. And it can be tripled only by using shared databases that will produce better information faster.

Third Requirement for Faster Decisions: Better Analysis

Faster and better information is a must, but it will be pointless if it is poorly analyzed and utilized. People who analyze information and use it to make decisions must be able to adapt to the new conditions. Top management should review the ability of its executives to evaluate information and make decisions that are not only faster but smarter. Then, next Monday morning, management should take the required actions—whether training, transfer, demotion, or early retirement.

You Must Be Able to Say "Sorry...Never Mind"

The ability to reverse a decision quickly is crucial today. When a company realizes it has made a mistake, it must not compound that with another mistake: hanging on stubbornly because of ego. Far better to cut your losses by acting next Monday morning to reverse the decision.

Case in Point: After committing the biggest marketing mistake in history (only the Edsel comes close), Coca-Cola quickly reversed itself and recovered superbly.

Coca-Cola's basic product—Coke—was losing out to Pepsi. Consumers seemed to prefer the taste of Pepsi, and Coca-Cola was becoming concerned. Preoccupied with the taste factor, Coca-Cola went out to test the market. After over 200,000 taste tests, results showed that the traditional Coke formula was losing 48 to 52 against Pepsi while a new Coke formula was winning 68 to 32.

Coca-Cola calculated that every percentage point was worth $300 million in sales. Understandably, it introduced New Coke—with a tremendous fanfare of advertising, publicity, and promotion. And it withdrew its traditional formula after 99 years.

Within weeks, Coca-Cola realized that it was facing a consumer revolt. In its preoccupation with taste, the company had overlooked the power of tradition. And it never found that out during its massive taste tests because it failed to ask the consumer: "How would you feel if the traditional Coke were to be taken away from you?"

But once Coca-Cola realized its error, it acted fast to reverse its decision. It admitted it had made a mistake and brought back the old Coke, renamed Coca-Cola Classic. Not easy, when you consider that the company had invested 4 years and many millions of dollars in the new Coke formula that it was sure would be a tremendous success.

In the end, Coca-Cola did better after its mistake than it had been doing before it. That was partly due to its quick reversal—and partly due to luck. During the hiatus of several weeks before it could come out with its new advertising for Coca-Cola Classic, it got so much free publicity from the media that its sales held up nicely.

In fact, some observers asked, "Wasn't the whole thing a Machiavellian scheme?" To which Coca-Cola President Donald R. Keough answered: "We are not that smart and we are not that dumb!"

Lesson to Be Learned

The ability to reverse a major decision without suffering fatal damage is an absolute necessity in today's unpredictable world. Let's say you figure there's only a 1 percent chance that your decision will be wrong—almost zero. If you cannot sustain the cost of reversing that decision, don't make it. Making a mistake from which you cannot recover is not worth taking a chance on—any kind of chance.

This doesn't mean a company should not make decisions that involve risk. Monsanto, for example, gambled some years ago on a new plastic called *acronitrile*. The company sold 50 percent of its output to bottlers for packaging soft drinks. Two months after Monsanto got into the business, the Food and Drug Administration ruled that the plastic was a possible carcinogen. Soft drink bottlers refused to buy any more of it, and Monsanto's *acronitrile* plants went out of the business at a cost of $300 million. A substantial sum, yes, but for Monsanto not a fatal blow. It was able to reverse its decision without affecting the future of the company.

On the other hand, Continental Illinois Bank failed to apply the "reversibility without catastrophe" test to its risky loans, and Union Carbide committed the same lapse when it determined its preventive—or, rather, nonpreventive—maintenance procedures.

Faster Decision Making: Get Started Now

Making decisions 3 times faster cannot be accomplished overnight. But it's important to get started now on your Monday morning actions. Here are some recommendations:

Monday Morning Actions

- Get started on overcoming computer illiteracy by learning to operate terminals and access databases. Use a small computer yourself, daily.
- Start networking within your organization by linking various departments and operations to common or shared databases.
- Develop a plan for expanding the electronic links to your field operations, key customers, and key suppliers.
- Promote the philosophy of shared databases and deal with the fears and insecurities of your key people.

- Develop criteria for calculating the cost of reversing a specific decision and for determining if that cost can be sustained.
- Evaluate the ability and willingness of your managers to make faster decisions.

TRIGGER POINT NINE

Shoot for zero turnover of your real, genuine 24-carat talent.

"It's difficult to soar like an eagle when you work with turkeys."

Author Unknown

"People are our most important asset" is probably the platitude most quoted by executives in speeches and annual reports—and it's true. It's also true that in actuality the majority of these executives mismanage their human resources in a most appalling way. It seems illogical, stupid, and counterproductive, but it happens all the time.

For a company to be successful in today's competitive, unpredictable world, it must act on a few simple truths:

1. Innovation is the key to growth—and only dedicated, motivated, unusually talented human beings can innovate.
2. Unless a company already has such truly talented people, it must find them. They are rare, so finding them isn't easy—but then you don't need many.

3. Your really talented people may only be 1 percent of your work force; but if they left, you would be in deep trouble.
4. Therefore, you must do everything necessary to hang on to your talented people—including giving them special treatment if they want it.

How to Find Out If You Have the Talented People You Need

There's a quick way to test whether you have those special, genuinely talented people you need for growth and success—the people with the rare ability to change the future of the enterprise. Without any preparation, write down the names of the individuals you can think of in your company who are so indispensable that they would create a disaster by leaving. (You might want to ask other managers to do the same thing.)

Even if only a few employees qualify, your company can consider itself very fortunate to have created an environment that fosters their development. But if no such list can be readily developed, there is an obvious need to procure talent. It must become a top-priority item, to be acted on next Monday morning.

Where does one find these rare people? Often they may already be in the company but their talent has gone unrecognized. That's why you need a formal talent inventory that will uncover them. You may find people who are capable of making significant, critical mass differences for the company.

The Three Capabilities You Must Look for—in One Employee

Some people are very good at detecting change. They have a very sensitive and accurate nose for smelling out new events, new markets, new opportunities. They are the detectives of change.

Other persons are superb planners. Given the new situation,

they can develop the necessary defensive and offensive moves, reallocate resources, and organize for action. They are the architects of change.

Others are the actual doers. They take the plans and implement them effectively. They are the agents of change.

What you should look for is that very rare, but very valuable, employee who embodies all three capabilities. This integrated dynamo is detective, architect, and agent of change in one person.

One good word to describe such an employee is *intrapreneur.* No innovative program can be started, funded, developed, implemented, and completed without a dedicated intrapreneur watching over it like a mother hen. It's not without peril. Many corporate toes and feelings will be stepped on and bruised in the process. Intrapreneurs risk their jobs every day. It's tough to live that way, particularly without the benefit of independent incomes.

Intrapreneurs should not simply be entrepreneurs who happen to be working inside a company. They should have a different blend of talents. The early entrepreneurs were stubborn individuals who had dreams and tremendous dedication. They were intuitive—"don't confuse me with the facts"—and often arbitrary and ruthless. Most giant companies of today were founded by such individuals. As the companies grew, the intuitive, do-it-themselves founders were replaced by professional managers. These were the technocrats, first armed with slide rules, then with computers. Reports, analyses, standards, and methods and operations manuals replaced gut feelings.

Today's intrapreneurs should be a blend of those extremes. Companies need strategists who can be defined as 50 percent inspiration and 50 percent perspiration—a blend of intuition and facts, innovation and derivation. Don't expect to turn a genuine entrepreneurial type into an intrapreneur with those qualities. Entrepreneurs want to be in business for themselves and won't stay long in salaried positions.

Intrapreneurs have most of the characteristics of the true entrepreneurs, but they like the security of regular incomes. They usually prefer small companies that can make faster decisions and provide a better opportunity for a future "fraction of the action." But even the larger companies have recognized the need for such people and are scurrying to attract them through a "small company atmosphere." This takes drastic restructuring:

- *Reorganization*—fewer levels, more delegated responsibilities
- *Divisionalization*—separate, fully integrated business units
- *Incentives*—profit sharing, bonuses, and stock ownership

IBM is a good example of a large company that nurtures its intrapreneurs. Despite its huge size, IBM has a caring attitude and innovative personnel practices. It promotes individuality, encourages innovation, and stimulates a continuous flow of new ideas and suggestions. High rewards prove that the company genuinely seeks and appreciates employee input. It listens.

Example: An interdisciplinary task force was organized to bring a new product to the market in 18 months instead of the normal 5 years. The group was organized and operated, according to a team member, "like a small independent business; we felt it was our own company and we acted accordingly."

You don't need an entrepreneur CEO to do this—and, in fact, such a CEO would be the wrong person to oversee an intrapreneurial system. The problem with creative, entrepreneurial CEOs is that they usually do all the innovating and risk taking themselves. The organization then pushes all tough decisions upstairs. An entrepreneur rarely develops intrapreneurs. The ideal CEO would be leader and motivator, with a rare ability to detect, attract, keep, and grow intrapreneurs in all parts of the business. The Chinese philospher Lao-Tse put it aptly over 2000 years ago:

> The leader is best when people barely know he exists. When his work is done, his aim is fulfilled, they will all say "We did this ourselves."

Keep Your Gorillas Happy

When you have some superbly talented people in your organization, you must do everything possible to hold on to them. They are the 2000-pound gorillas. How do you keep gorillas happy? You give them what they want.

Your gorillas can be difficult to manage. They tend to be stubborn and opinionated, full of idiosyncrasies and disruptive habits. But whatever their faults and maladjustments, they have to be tolerated, supported, encouraged, and loved. Whatever the gorillas want, they should get. Because they are worth it.

A conventional VP of personnel will point out that it's unfair, that other employees will complain and resent such preferential treatment. Your answer should be: So what? Brilliant performers and exceptional producers are entitled to exceptional treatment. Your policy should read: "Good rewards for good services; extraordinary rewards for extraordinary services."

Actually, most employees understand and accept that a major difference in performance justifies different rewards and privileges. Their morale is not affected if the criteria are fair and openly communicated.

So even if you have to battle your personnel VP, give your gorillas what they want. A gorilla gets away with anything. Two examples:

1. An exceptionally talented engineer had an unusual request. He wanted an original Picasso for his cubicle (he didn't even have an office). A million-dollar Picasso? Now that's difficult. However, the engineer's boss discovered that New York's Museum of Modern Art rents paintings to companies. So for $5000 a year, the engineer was provided with the Picasso he wanted. His employer has no regrets—he has been phenomenally productive.

2. A gorilla was offered a bonus of $10,000 for outstanding work. But this gorilla said he'd rather not have the money—because when he brought the check home, his wife would probably want to spend it on something he didn't particularly want, like a car. "Instead of money, give me a trip to Europe," the gorilla suggested. "The airline tickets, hotel reservations, traveler's checks." That way, he could go home and say, "Honey, we're going to Europe," and there wouldn't be a thing she could do about it.

It made sense to his boss, since it wouldn't cost the company any more. But the personnel VP raised all kinds of objections: It would set a precedent; everyone would want an exception; we're not in the travel business. The gorilla's boss had to pound the desk to get what he wanted.

Unfortunately, companies often fail to recognize the value of their talented people—and lose them. Even a well-managed company like IBM has such lapses. Most notably, it failed to give its brilliant programmer, Gene Amdahl, gorilla treatment. So Amdahl left IBM and formed his own company, which became a $300 million operation.

One of the worst things a company can do is offer inadequate rewards for extraordinary contributions, but it happens all the time. Here's a typical example, reprinted from Pratt & Whitney's company publication:

> John C. Winfree, assistant engineer at Pratt, has submitted eleven suggestions that saved the company $730,128. Winfree actually made thirty-two suggestions last year; fourteen of his ideas are still being reviewed. Under the company's employee incentive program, Pratt awarded Winfree $4,000 for his winning suggestions.

A measly $4000 for suggestions that saved the company almost a million dollars! My recommendation for companies that want to inspire innovation by their employees is to give an employee a check for half of the first year's savings generated by an adopted idea. In Winfree's case, $350,000. That's a great attention getter, especially when it's publicized in the company's house organ.

You Need Flexible Policies to Hold on to Your Talented People

It is a serious mistake to attempt to create a homogeneous group of alike personalities and behavior to achieve a smooth-running organization. The result will be a placid mediocrity, because your really talented people won't tolerate such an environment. They will leave. Future success is much better served by encouraging diversity, bringing together different personalities, and providing opportunities for constructive conflict. Don't expect anything original from an echo.

To hold on to their talented people, companies must make their personnel policies increasingly flexible. The melting pot of assimilated personalities that has prevailed in the past has given way to a high level of individualism that must be accommodated with a varied menu—a smorgasbord of financial and nonfinancial rewards, incentives, and benefits.

This need is especially crucial because so many thousands of middle managers have lost their jobs in recent years. In a study reported in *The New York Times* of February 10, 1987, the Hay Group, a consulting firm, pointed out that the ones that remain are cynical and pessimistic. Yet these are the key, talented people who must be motivated to produce the outstanding performance of which they are capable.

Hay found that "for the first time in the history of our surveys, fewer than half the middle managers took a favorable view about their opportunities for advancement." In addition, only about 60 percent of the managers surveyed felt secure about their jobs, "a massive drop from over 80 percent just 10 years before."

True, said the Hay report, insecurity can lead to increased productivity—but it can also create hostility and make the employee eager to accept any job that opens up in another company.

What's the answer? Your company needs a focused program to hold on to talented people by:

1. Furnishing specialized training
2. Providing individual motivation
3. Offering rapid advancement opportunities

Check your personnel practices to see if you pay special attention to intrapreneurial talent:

- Do you provide a "fraction of the action?" Can your intrapreneurs get rich?
- Do you have a flat, horizontal organization for faster promotions?

- Do you provide cafeteria-style benefits so people can choose the kinds of benefits they want?
- Do you counsel and help your talented elite with special education, training, self-improvement, and computer support?
- How many are added yearly to your talent inventory?
- Is this endeavor monitored by the CEO—or by a glorified clerk-bureaucrat?

Monday Morning Actions

- Write down (and ask your associates to write down) a list of 5 to 10 individuals—at any level of the organization—who are so knowledgeable and talented that it would be a major blow to the company if one of them left.
- If you don't have enough indispensable people on the list, get started on analyzing and improving the climate, the motivation, and the reward system in your company. Make it priority 1.
- If you don't have a formal talent inventory, start one—and include employees at every level.
- Consider how your organization can be restructured, if necessary, to create a better environment for innovative intrapreneurs to work in.
- Review your list of indispensable employees—and ask yourself if they are getting the special rewards they deserve and want.

PART FOUR

Five Tools for Triggering Action Next Monday Morning

"It is important to make certain that our efforts are directed at the decisive core of the problem, and not on distracting side issues. The more complex the difficulties we face, the more important it becomes to bear this in mind, for it is human nature to try to evade what we cannot cope with."

BERNARD BARUCH

This book is devoted to one basic objective: Monday morning actions. But not just any Monday morning actions. Action without thought won't produce the results you want. Behind every Monday morning action there must be a concept, a philosophy, a carefully thought out objective.

Basically, it's a macro-to-micro thought process. It starts with an overall concept or objective and from that develops a series of derivatives that lead finally to specific Monday morning action.

It's not that difficult to do if you have the right tools. That's what we're going to talk about now.

Pyramid thinking

Pyramid thinking is a powerful management decision-making tool. It is an ideal way to implement macro-to-micro derivative thinking, make a decision, and start an action next Monday morning.

The top of the pyramid is reserved for basic concepts, key general factors, or priority objectives. Working your way down to the bottom of the pyramid identifies the specific actions necessary to begin the implementation.

The best way to explain pyramid thinking is through examples.

Example 1: A Small Printing Company

Top-of-the-pyramid objective	Faster growth.
First derivative	More sales.
Second derivative	Marketing vs. order taking.
Third derivative	Offer a service requiring printing as a by-product.
Fourth derivative	Monthly follow-up of customers/prospects in various businesses.
Fifth derivative	Select automobile dealers; offer database maintenance for their car-service customers with printing and mailing of personalized reminders, service and sales specials, brochures, etc.

Sixth derivative	Action next Monday morning: sign up the first car dealer in the neighborhood.

Example 2: An Automobile Giant

Top-of-the-pyramid concept	Fight competition.
First derivative	Japanese competition and internal competition.
Second derivative	(*a*) Make a better car than Toyota; (*b*) reduce competition between GM divisions such as Buick vs. Oldsmobile.
Third derivative	(*a*) Toyota is hard to beat, so better join them; (*b*) reorganize GM divisions.
Fourth derivative	(*a*) Joint venture with Toyota; (*b*) establish three noncompeting GM divisions: popular car (Chevrolet), fun car (Pontiac, Corvette), and luxury car (Cadillac, Olds, Buick).
Fifth derivative	(*a*) Protect Toyota deal with a second line of defense: joint venture with Daewoo Motor Company of South Korea; (*b*) establish in the United States a separate budget-car GM unit (Saturn).

Example 3: A Slipper Manufacturer

Top-of-the-pyramid concept	Diversification.
First derivative	Must be done from strength; thus related to shoes.
Second derivative	Shoes as a category is too general. Specialize. Find a niche.
Third derivative	Focus on major social changes to discover specialized needs and markets. Increase in number of working women is major social change.
Fourth derivative	What kinds of shoes does a working woman want and need? She wants them to be comfortable but stylish.
Fifth derivative	How do you satisfy each requirement? (*a*) Style can be provided by an Italian designer and (*b*) comfort by new shoe technology.

Sixth derivative	Monday morning actions: (*a*) Fly to Italy, pirate best designer, and (*b*) initiate patent and license search for new foot-support technology. (Result of search: small plastic hollow balls filled with air and liquid, embedded in the sole and heel of new shoe to reduce fatigue.)

In Example 3, the follow-through (financing, manufacturing, distribution, marketing, advertising, franchising), while obviously extremely important, falls into the category of normal business. The creative part is the macro-to-micro sequence—from a broad market category to new-product specifications of style and comfort and solutions for those specifications.

Many readers may react to these examples of pyramid thinking with uneasiness and incredulity. Pyramid thinking may seem to be a broad oversimplification. It is not. It is a serious technique for reducing large masses of thought and data to the absolute key essentials. It is a distillation process to get the essence and then expand from there.

This requires genuine support and encouragement from top management. It must be done, with finesse, in an environment conducive to innovative thinking. Participants must be willing to express themselves freely and to constructively argue pros and cons of each item on the agenda. Above all, it requires talented and innovative people. Without them, the process could produce a disastrous series of wrong conclusions and decisions.

Directed brainstorming

Pyramid thinking can, of course, be done by an individual manager, but it can also be done by a group. Perhaps it is most effective as a group activity, because the interaction can produce the best action proposals and result in a mutual commitment to actually implementing the proposals.

This is crucially important. Ideas without implementation are sterile seeds that never grow. This book has repeatedly stressed the necessity for fast, decisive action. Unfortunately, actions that affect the future and those based on uncertain, often obscure and controversial clues tend to be postponed. It is easier to respond to loudly resounding fire alarms.

What's needed is a formal group process for fostering ideas *and* implementing them next Monday morning. Directed brainstorming is such a process. It has been tested over a period of years with managers in various enterprises of all sizes and diversities of fields. The process is practical; it produces good, often extraordinary results. Here's how it works:

Prerequisites

Assemble five to seven managers in a comfortably furnished living room with a semicircular sofa. Disconnect the telephone. Provide four easels with plenty of pads, masking tape, and felt-tipped multicolored markers. Have lots of coffee and soft drinks.

The purpose of this environment is to stimulate a free exchange of ideas and opinions. More positive results can be achieved in one or two days of intensive concentration than in months of conventional procedures and meetings. The moderator must remain quite neutral and noncontroversial but be able to ask penetrating questions and direct traffic. The CEO should be present but must try to behave as an equal participant, not the all-knowing, dominating authority figure.

Phase 1: Factors

The participants name and list the many factors that have potential direct or indirect effects on a chosen topic—a problem or opportunity, a key platitude, or any top-of-the-pyramid key word. Examples:

- Diversification
- New products
- Automation
- Motivation
- Organization
- Entrepreneurship
- Going public
- Going private
- Government regulations
- Executive succession

There should be at least 50 to 100 factors thrown in and jotted on the easel pads. The rules forbid discussion during the listing of the factors; anything goes.

If participants fail to come up with forces that are affecting the subject at hand, one of two possible reasons may be responsible:

1. The managers do not feel free to express themselves frankly and openly—indicating a one-man rule and dictatorial culture.
2. They genuinely can't think of many factors relating to the topic—perhaps symptoms of an inbred and shallow intellectual level. However, even such negatives can provide a valuable insight to the CEO or the highest executive present.

Phase 2: Potential Impact

With several easel pads filled with positive or negative factors affecting a given topic, the participants can now engage in a spirited discussion of the relative impact of each of the factors. For instance, the ratings can vary from a −3 to a +3.

Differences of opinion should not only be heard but encouraged. Constructive conflict is healthy and is part of the process. It's particularly worthwhile when one manager rates a factor a high minus while another judges it to be a high plus.

Critics of directed brainstorming argue that such discussions are often based on feelings and intuition rather than on hard facts; thus, any conclusions reached are dangerous because they may contradict reality. To avoid that possibility, the managers chosen should be knowledgeable in their fields. In addition, a prudent CEO can have the conclusions of the brainstorming meeting checked for accuracy of facts and data by an independent source.

Phase 3: Priority of Factors

After the factors are rated on their relative impact and a consensus is reached on each subject, the next step is additional refinement. The top-rated positive factors and negative factors must now be ranked according to their impact and importance. This requires careful analysis and even more thoughtful discussion.

The final result is a specific priority list that becomes the basis for selecting actions to remedy or exploit the situation. Such a rating is clearly very sensitive and must be decided upon with plenty of input and consideration from all participants.

Phase 4: Possible Actions

The directed brainstorming process enters a new phase by asking the participants to make Monday morning implementation proposals on the priority items that were selected in phase 3:

- What new and different innovative actions could be undertaken?
- Why weren't they started before?
- Are there other, underlying reasons for not acting on items given such a high priority by the company's top executives?
- Are there policies that must be changed?
- Is the organization structure faulty? Was the problem ignored? Are opportunities being lost? Why, why, why?
- What additional actions should be taken to ensure that top-priority factors are handled as part of the normal course of business operations?

Phase 4 should produce a list of potential actions to cover items on the priority list and additional, often more important, actions to improve the basic decision-making structure of the company—such as reorganization, delegation, powers reserved, redefinition of responsibilities, change of objectives, and business priorities.

Phase 5: Priority of Actions

The group now has before it a menu of action proposals. The final stage of the process is to select, in strict priority order, the key actions to be initiated next Monday morning. Frank discussion and constructive conflict are again desirable. The availability of funds and human resources must be considered. Previous priorities may have to be revised.

The crucial point of the session finally emerges. What are the three or four absolutely most important actions that must be undertaken within the business, starting Monday morning?

Directed brainstorming is effective because it reduces general platitudes to practical, down-to-earth, "what must be done Monday morning" actions. The listing of those actions, also in priority order, becomes a de facto strategic plan for the corporation.

The key to this management blueprint is its incompleteness. Only the important or, even better, absolutely *most* important, issues should be considered and resolved. The others will take care of themselves. Top-management attention should not be diverted by whether to plant begonias or petunias in the company parking lot—or even by the amount of office space that may be needed 5 years hence. These matters will be resolved somehow; they are not essential issues, even if administrative bureaucrats claim otherwise.

On the other hand, once a top-priority list of issues is prepared, every sentence made must be cross-referenced by a Monday morning action proposal. Otherwise, directed brainstorming remains sterile and has no significance to the business. The most important executive question to any statement of a problem or opportunity is "What are we going to do about it?" You know when!

The process works. Its simplicity is deceiving; the results are often extraordinary.

TOOL THREE

Razor blade reading and clue management

Ideas and concepts for innovation and uniqueness are usually inspired by external events and subtle changes in the external environment. The fact is that most major innovations in a particular industry originate outside that industry. The microwave oven developed from military contracts with Raytheon, not from the work of the home-appliance industry. Most IBM innovations did not come from IBM or even the computer industry; they came from the communications industry.

Keep in mind that you can't control your own future. Your destiny is not in your hands; it is in the hands of the irrational consumer and society. The changes in their needs, desires, and demands will tell you where you must go.

All this means that managers must themselves feel the pulse of change on a daily, continuous basis. To rely on expert opinion and on consensus is to rely on conventional wisdom and the law of averages. This is not conducive to innovation because it is tied closely to the status quo.

So managers should become socioeconomic crystal ball gazers themselves. They should have intense curiosity, observe events, analyze trends, seek the clues of change, and translate those clues into opportunities.

One practical, tested method for doing this is *razor blade reading*. Here's how it works:

Reading Process

Don't depend on print or audio clipping services—they do your thinking for you. Instead, subscribe to at least 30 magazines covering fields in which you are interested. Have them come to your home, because if you have a boss, it really doesn't look too good when you've got 30 magazines on your desk and you're reading them.

Don't read the magazines—scan them. And scan them yourself. Don't delegate razor blade reading to your secretary, because after a year you will have a very knowledgeable secretary and you won't know a damn thing. However, if you have a big company, you could get four or five people to take 10 different topics each and do their own razor blade reading. Once every 2 months, get together for dinner, have a little wine, and exchange views.

When do you have time to read magazines? You'd be surprised at how many opportunities you have: early morning, at night before you go to sleep (I find that the *Journal of Petroleum Statistics* is better than a sleeping pill), in the bathroom, waiting in line, while you're traveling. Whatever you read, ask yourself:

- Can it affect my business?
- What problem may it create?
- What opportunity may it create?

Clipping Process

Whenever a piece of information triggers a potential connection with your business, cut out the item with a razor blade (or suitable substitute that you always carry with you). Don't hesitate to mutilate your newspapers and periodicals—then throw them away. Don't keep useless information. And don't read for "later reference." Clip immediately and date the clipping.

Filing Process

Establish no more than 10 files in ordinary manila folders, each representing a key interest or area of responsibility in your business. Some examples:

- Overall economic trends
- Taxation
- International trade
- Status of competition
- Raw material costs
- Capital costs
- Wage costs
- Union settlements
- Productivity
- Quality
- Personnel
- Motivation
- Automation
- Robotics
- High tech
- Computers
- Bonds

Every day, file your clippings in the appropriate folders to create chronological series of data, information, and clues on the particular subjects.

Analysis Process

Review each file once a month. You'll find that it can be a revelation. When new things begin to happen, you find references to them in many different sources. When you put all the bits and pieces together and review them, you can see a definite trend, whether opportunity or threat. You know something is happening, and that's your trigger point for corporate action. Just 6 months ahead is all you need to beat the competition.

Action Process

Razor blade reading is useless unless it leads to a decision and action. This is the final test of the real value of the process. Will it generate better decisions and trigger earlier actions to exploit new opportunities or solve or prevent potential problems? Try it and see.

Pick your own reading material according to your specific interests, but a good basis for getting started is the carefully selected list you'll find at the end of the book. For daily coverage, *The Wall Street Journal* is essential. Another outstanding newspaper is *The Financial Times of London,* which has a high-technology communication system for early distribution in major U.S. cities. *Business Week* and *U.S. News & World Report* are excellent weeklies, and an informative biweekly is *The Economist.* Among monthlies, *Fortune, Forbes,* and *INC* stand out, and an indispensable quarterly is

Razor Blade Reading in the Sky

I subscribe to 120 magazines—and scan them all. (I don't recommend this for busy executives, however.) Since I also fly a lot, I combine the two activities to get much of my reading done in the air. Flight attendants see me stagger on board with about 30 pounds of magazines—and then walk off at the end of the flight without any. They're neatly stacked up on my seat—all I'm carrying is a small bundle of clippings. It works well. One thing I've learned, though, is to cut my address label out of each magazine. I've done that ever since a friend called me and said he'd found a stack of magazines I'd accidentally left behind on an airplane seat—and he was sending them all back to me.

Quarterly Economic Outlook U.S.A., put out by the University of Michigan.

For statistical reference material, the U.S. government is the most prolific source. Some useful monthly publications are *Economic Indicators, Survey of Current Business, Business Conditions Digest,* and *Monthly Labor Review.* For annual statistics, consult the *U.S. Statistical Abstract* (Commerce Department) and the *Economic Report of the President,* available from the Government Printing Office.

TOOL FOUR

Gap analysis

What manager doesn't know that planning is one of the essential functions of management? Yet, while planning may be given plenty of lip service and publicity in annual reports, its importance and practice have actually deteriorated in the recent years of fast change and constant crises. This is unfortunate, because planning should be increased and be made more sophisticated when the status quo is disturbed.

However, managers are often afraid of planning or, perhaps, just find it distasteful. Frequently, the reason is that a doer feels uncomfortable performing a "soft" activity: it deals with the future; its conclusions cannot be proved until it's too late; there are no standard methods of implementation; it takes time away from pressing daily tasks. A prevalent managerial attitude is demonstrated by the facetious but revealing statement: "Any damn fool can plan five years ahead, but it takes real executive ability to leap daily from crisis to crisis."

One solution to this attitude is to abolish planning, not as a function, but as a word. An enterprise does not need planning; it needs managing. Particularly, managing for the future or, even more precisely, managing the future. Today's strategies are tomorrow's results. We should stop using the word "planning" and replace it with the term "strategic management." Strategic management connotes taking proper, innovative, clever actions—next Monday morning—to assure the continuous success and unfaltering progress of the corporation.

A major criticism of planning activities is that it takes too much time to procure and analyze data before a recommendation is made or a plan is prepared. The obvious answer is to manage in the practical zone between paralysis by analysis and flying by the seat of one's pants.

How do you achieve a happy medium? Pyramid thinking and directed brainstorming can help. But perhaps the most powerful tool in strategic management is *gap analysis.* Gap analysis is a clear-cut, step-by-step procedure that can effectively help an organization respond successfully to changing external trends and at the same time reach desired goals.

What Do We Mean by "Gap"?

The Greek letter *delta* is used in mathematics to signify difference. It can also be a useful symbol in business planning. The definition of change is the difference between two states: before and after the fact. The first step in planning, or any management function, is to understand the dynamics of change. What happened; what is happening; what will happen?

The focus must be on the *delta* of the event. This difference creates a gap between the old and the new situation. The gap must be filled, solved, or dissolved—it cannot remain untouched because the status quo, the fine equilibrium, has been upset.

Example: When integrated circuits replaced wires and vacuum tubes, the maintenance and repairs of electronic equipment changed drastically. This created a *delta*—a significant difference between what service people knew and what they had to know. To fill this major gap of knowledge and methodology, service people had to be retrained and taught new methods of handling repairs.

Gaps cannot be filled by wishing or hoping. They must be filled by forceful, innovative actions. A *delta* spurs good management to prompt action.

Another Example: The development of smaller, cheaper dish antennas has created a *delta* for cable companies. Pay channels such as HBO can be received directly by dish antennas, bypassing the rental of converters from the cable company. The gap of lost revenue must be filled immediately, before the practice spreads. Expensive scrambling of satellite signals and local detection of illegal signal reception are being considered. One thing is certain: The cable companies' status quo has been disturbed and the companies must eliminate the *delta,* even though that will be expensive and complex.

Just as important, gap analysis can also be used to reach desired goals. To do that, one establishes a willful *delta* between a dream objective and today's actual results, the business-as-usual status quo. The gap can be filled only by new, innovative actions specifically aimed at the *delta.*

There is nothing very new about the mechanics of the gap analysis process. The success comes from the methodical and dedicated application of a thinking discipline. It needs top leadership to motivate and maintain it.

Some Basic Deltas *You Must Consider*

Strategic management is less difficult than the preceding pages may make it appear, because the process is relative, not absolute. Management doesn't have to seek perfection—it only has to beat the competition. In that battle, the margin of superiority should be just enough to win; 10 percent is a good rule-of-thumb figure. Bigger differences are expensive to achieve and don't bring any greater benefits.

Initiate this relativistic approach with an extensive analysis of all your competitors, direct and indirect. This should be done before anything else. Knowledge of one's customer, one's market, and one's competition is the foundation of strategic management.

The *deltas* of competition, the key positive and negative comparisons and factors, must be carefully identified and placed in priority order. What are the most crucial differences to be overcome (negative) or maintained (positive)? What new actions must be taken next Monday morning?

It's a very basic and straightforward process. It's also a neglected one. The lack of solid competitive analysis is appalling, particularly in companies with plenty of resources to keep continuous tabs on their competition rather than make periodic efforts.

Another key *delta* of knowledge is against the "leading edge." The key question to ask and answer is: "Who in the world has the most advanced techniques and practices in marketing, production, R&D, data processing, automation, service, personnel, financial?" And: "How do these companies compare and relate to ours?"

The obvious first step is to acquire information. Managers must be knowledgeable about worldwide practices relevant to their operations. To be that knowledgeable requires serious study of various and different ways of doing business. That prevents inbreeding, arrogance, and the ostrich complex. The next step is doing something about improving one's operations. Not some day in the future, but next Monday morning.

What Factors Must Be Considered in Strategic Management?

The scope of strategic planning and management is defined in an interesting fashion by William F. Martz, coauthor of the *Corporate Planning Process Manual*. He describes the various forces that impact on an organization and must be dealt with in a comprehensive planning effort:

The Shapers: The social, economic, governmental factors that shape society, the consumer, and the economy. They create new and different market conditions, and determine...

The Demanders: The specific markets that demand to be served and wait to be fulfilled by...

The Satisfiers: The products and services, properly designed and priced, ready to satisfy the specific market demand. Satisfiers are the target of...

The Challengers: New technology—threatening rapid obsolescence of existing products—and competition trying to secure a larger share of the market. They can be conquered by...

The Generators: The operations and supply phases of the business—they provide the development and manufacturing of products, the selling efforts, and all the other activities required to bring a product or a service to the marketplace. The generators are fueled by...

The Energizers: The human resources needed to make it all happen—talented, motivated, trained, skilled, and innovative people and physical resources—the financial means and facilities such as buildings, plants, and equipment. Finally, there are...

The Feeders: The suppliers of all the external resources required to support the internal effort. They become increasingly important as companies subcontract more and become critically dependent on the efficiency of their feeders. The feeders must provide timely delivery, good quality, and the right price. They are of vital importance to the entire process and should be given more attention and supervision in an era of deteriorating service and quality and just-in-time inventory requirements.

Plan Only What's Important—and Have Fun

Gap analysis planning should not be a complicated, tedious chore. It should be a creative, interesting, fun endeavor with the enthusiastic participation of key managers throughout the company. Planning must be useful to the company; the process must make a definite, direct, major contribution to the continuity/futurity of the business. It must be perceived as one of the success factors of the enterprise.

To earn this mark of distinction, planning must deal with important factors only. Low-priority issues and routine matters must be deliberately ignored and bypassed. Company management should treat planning as a prime mover, not as an activity dealing with the obvious and the trivial.

On the following pages you will find the step-by-step procedures for conducting a gap analysis. The analysis should be made by profit center rather than by one analysis for the entire organization.

And remember: Plans should be short! The key to effective strategic management is to distill plans down to the essentials of absolute importance.

Step 1. Where Are We? External Environment Profile

Understanding the external environment relating to your business is more than important, it's vital. Step 1 of gap analysis deals with the reality of the present.

What Are the Key Factors in Our Environment—and How Much Can We Control Them?

You want to position your business within the present external realities. You seek to better understand your markets, your customers, your distribution channels, and your products and services. Here are some guidelines:

- Prepare the profiles carefully and thoughtfully.
- Concentrate on the important areas.
- Reduce the amount of information to eliminate noncritical mass data and relations.
- Attempt to isolate the key factors that comprise the lifeblood of your company.
- Summarize and establish priorities.
- Determine the degree of control or influence you have over the key external factors you have isolated and prioritized.
- Transform all important summary data into quantitative terms so that they are measurable and amenable to control and comparison.
- Try to convert even qualitative statements into some sort of quantified ranking or comparative scale. Effective planning largely depends on the ability to measure ostensibly unmeasurable factors.
- Prepare graphs to reflect your key factors visually.

Step 2. Where Are We? Internal Environment Profile

Objectivity Is a Must

It is usually easier to be objective in dealing with the external forces outside your control than with internal factors that are under management direction and were created by managerial decisions. However, it is essential to examine internal operations with objectivity, even if you were the main orchestrator of past performance. Unemotional frankness in analyzing internal situations is an important prerequisite of a good planning process.

Where Are We Right Now?

You want to take detailed snapshots of your business activities as they are in the present. Prepare a series of internal environment profiles. These should cover today's activities in the areas of technology, human resources, physical resources, finances, and top-management philosophy.

The sum of all activities and attitudes helps to define the nature of your present business. By carefully examining the various functional profiles, you can acquire a list of the key issues that face the business in both the short and long terms.

Setting Priorities

We have repeatedly stressed the importance of prioritizing. It's the main and best tool for achieving better planning and operating results, because it forces constant evaluation, risk determination, and the calculation of relative value and impact. It makes managers think—and concentrate their efforts on important items. Do not hesitate to remind your people at all levels to manage by established priorities and to bring forcefully and rapidly to top management's attention any actual or suggested changes in priorities.

Wait—It's Not Time to Plan Ahead Yet

When you have completed steps 1 and 2, you should know where you are today. Obviously, past history and past trends are informative and provide background, knowledge, and an explanation of your present position. But yesterday and even today are not necessarily the harbingers of tomorrow. Don't extrapolate yet.

Step 3. Where Are We Going? Future External Environment

You Must Consider the Impact of Future External Factors

External forces not under management's control exert a growing impact on the operations of any enterprise. Because this is an era of flux and unpredictability, external forces change more rapidly and more drastically. The new impacts may create widely different effects from those inventoried in step 1.

You can't know what's going to happen in the future, but you must still make assumptions about the key forces of tomorrow. This is not a one-time, static analysis. It must become a continuous, dynamic search and analysis process—refining, adjusting, rethinking.

Catalog Future Influences Systematically

It is first necessary to collect and catalog the major potential future influences on the company's business. Judgment and creative evaluation must be used with a touch of intuition and speculation. The main task, however, is to try to state, in order of importance, the direct or indirect effects of the changing factors on specific areas of your business. It requires making risk decisions on the priority, the kind, and the magnitude of the impact.

It is not an easy task, but it is a very important one. Proper understanding and, to a certain degree, guesstimating of future marketplace opportunities help in designing new and better products or services—and thus make a difference between success and failure. Together they are your most important foundation for protecting and building the future.

Know Your Key Challenges and Threats

There is a constant need for review, consolidation, and synthesis. This is true not only of planning but also of most thoughtful activities. One should pause and reflect: What are the critical elements of a situation?

Listing the key challenges and threats is of crucial importance. If properly thought out, the list constitutes a springboard for investigation, validation, and, ultimately, initiation of an entire array of important action programs to assure the continuity/futurity of the enterprise. Obviously, the original list had better be valid and properly balanced; otherwise, many subsequent steps will be costly and ineffective.

Step 4. Where Can We Go? Capabilities

Vast ideas with half-vast resources are incompatible with reality. An organization should at all times have a down-to-earth understanding of its capabilities.

Do You Know Your Strengths and Needs?

A thorough analysis of one's strengths and needs is a classical recommendation of any book on management and planning. It is still the right approach as long as it's done in a detached, unbiased, factual manner.

Think through why your enterprise is still in business. It obviously must be doing something right. What are the key success factors that have contributed to your progress and growth up to now? Make a further inventory of your strengths and needs (a euphemism for weaknesses) in your major business functions such as marketing, production, R&D, personnel, finance, and administration. Be selective—list in priority order only the important strengths and critical needs. Don't clutter your mind and your limited time with trivial nits.

Check Your Key Result and Activity Areas

To supplement your analysis of strengths and needs according to function, analyze the strengths and needs by key result and activity areas as well. Over 20 years ago, Peter Drucker and General Electric determined that a successful company must possess significant strengths in seven crucial areas. That is still very true today.

Carefully check your real capabilities and performance under each of these headings. Are there any serious shortcomings? Are there certain unique abilities? The key result and activity areas are:

- Customer satisfaction
- Productivity
- Innovation
- Management development
- Employee attitudes
- Public responsibility
- Continuity/futurity

Place all your strengths and needs in perspective, in relation to future requirements of the business. Weigh, analyze, compare. Make a final short list of your key strengths and needs. Learn to operate by priorities. No business can exploit all the opportunities or correct all the deficiencies. The art of successful managing is to select the most important factors and to act upon them with single-minded, determined purpose.

Feeders Analysis—More Important Than Ever

Today's companies are subcontracting more, adopting just-in-time inventory, going in for joint ventures. Any business is dependent to a large degree on external sources: raw and semiprocessed materials, manufacturing or assembly subcontracts, engineering or specialized consulting services, financial help, distribution channels, scarce talent. Clearly, you must analyze your strengths and needs in this area as well as internally.

Evaluate your position with each essential external purveyor of goods and services with which you have a relationship. How good are they to you, how reliable, how dependent are you on any one of them? What are your alternatives, secondary sources, in-house emergency capabilities?

Feeders analysis is an important task, because the activities are not under the company's direct control. Don't neglect it.

Step 5. Where Might We Go? Future Internal Environment

The business of business is to serve selected markets with wanted products and services. There is a continuous need to match the demands of the various market segments with the satisfiers (products and services) offered by the enterprise. Management must analyze and project the outlook for its present output on both a short- and a long-term basis. The purpose is to determine the viability of present business-as-usual operations in light of the changing conditions of tomorrow.

Forecasts versus Potentials: A Crucial Comparison

Potentials are estimates of total demand of all the markets for all the products and services. Sales forecasts are projected company sales of products and services in the company's market segment. The difference between potentials and forecasts is a very significant indicator of future trends.

If the company's share of the market segment is large and the potential is not growing, gaining additional share will be difficult and costly. New markets and new products and services must be developed.

If the company's share is small, additional penetration should be possible, regardless of the long-range trend of the total potential or the short-term outlook of the economy. While penetration of market from 1 percent to 2 percent may compute to 100 percent growth, the overall effect is small. The effort is under the company's control and is not significantly affected by external factors. This is obviously not so when the firm has 60 percent or even 30 percent of the market segment share.

Extrapolations versus New Conditions: Another Vital Comparison

An additional tool for analyzing market and product and service growth potential is the comparison of two trends: extrapolation of growth based on past performance vs. change in future growth resulting from the impact of new conditions and new external forces. If the new-conditions trend exceeds the extrapolation, prospects are evidently brighter than if the reverse is projected. Serious and thoughtful analysis is required. Present size of the market share plays an important role in the company's determination of future prospects.

Assessing the Future Business Situation

Evaluating future market attractiveness and product and service vitality sets two important parameters for future planning. It determines both the minimum, conservative base of business as usual and the new prospects of where and how high present business could grow in changing conditions. It sets the stage for establishing challenging objectives for the future, the next step in gap analysis.

Step 6. Where Do We Want to Go? Objectives

We examined the present and future environments, the momentum of business as usual, the probable changes in the market, and product and service potentials and forecasts. We analyzed our capabilities, present and future, and critically examined our strengths and our needs. Now—and only now—it's time to set our goals and objectives. We must state explicitly where we really want to go.

Match Objectives with Personality

Setting objectives should be an emotional experience. Objectives must reflect the inner ambitions and desires of the power person—that is, whoever is really in charge, whether it's the CEO, the chairman, the largest stockholder, the banker. This person must balance company objectives with inner personal drives. A conservative banker wouldn't adapt to the high-risk, supergrowth objectives of a new venture, and an ambitious go-go entrepreneur wouldn't stand for the dull, secure objectives of a mature, plodding company.

Establish a Pyramid of Objectives

A corporate plan requires an entire hierarchy of interrelated objectives. The pyramid of objectives starts with overall business growth wants: a statement of key values, markets, products and services, unique capabilities, and the level of profitability the corporation wishes to attain. Basic quantitative goals of sales volume, net profits, and return on investment are summarized and extended into the future. Desired improvement should be explicitly stated for each of the seven key result and activity areas. The same thing must be done for the unique capabilities considered essential in marketing, production, R&D, human resources, finance, and administration.

Redefine Your Business

The definition of the nature of your present business should be compared with the definition of the nature of your future business. If the corporate objectives are challenging and meaningful, there will be a substantial difference between the two statements. This difference creates the stimulus for new strategies and innovative action programs.

Set Functional Objectives

Once overall objectives have been established, use them as a basis for setting departmental and functional objectives. Functional planning in each department provides the vehicle for goal setting in each major function of the company.

Why Objective Setting Is Vital

Clear, precise, quantitative objectives create and cement the structure within which a solid planning process can be instituted. They provide an unequivocal reference base for comparison and evaluation of actual results. They also serve as catalysts for and stimulators of continuous efforts to improve overall and individual performance.

Step 7. What Do We Have to Do? Gap Setting

You are now ready to start setting gaps. These gaps will represent the differences between the arbitrarily established objectives of "where do we want to go" (step 6) and projections of what will happen if you stick to "business as usual" (step 5). The latter projections, representing "where we might go," are not mere extrapolations; they are trends carefully adjusted by taking into consideration the impact of new external forces and assumptions of future changes in the environment (step 3).

Gaps Are a Powerful Tool

A comprehensive set of precise, quantitative, and measurable gaps is an extremely powerful planning and implementing tool for management at any level. It can be successfully used by any organization, whether a profit-oriented corporation, a not-for-profit institution, a government agency, or a charitable organization. Gaps are easy to understand and easy to communicate. They have a common language, and they convey a simple message: "We must do something to fill the gap in order to achieve our goals."

Gaps Can Be Used by Everyone

The concept of a measurable gap can be applied in a pyramid fashion throughout the organization. The Board of Directors and the CEO may be interested in filling a net profit after taxes gap. The VP of marketing sees that gap as one in volume of sales. The sales director views the gap as numbers of salespeople and their qualifications (gap in training or, perhaps, motivation and incentives). The R&D director views the gap as the number of new products, often because of gaps in technological advances. The manufacturing executive examines the gap in the light of per unit production costs, created partly by the gap in quality control and the gap in efficient automation of production facilities.

Lower in the organization, a shipping clerk may wish to solve the gap of unfulfilled delivery schedules, while a salesman struggles with the gap in his monthly quota. In other words, gaps can be used on individual planning and implementing levels as well as on corporate, divisional, or departmental/functional levels.

Taking the Shame Out of Gaps

The existence of gaps in an organization is not a shameful or undesirable situation. Gaps are created on purpose and with a purpose. One of the important roles of a good planning process is to encourage the creation of challenging gaps. This provides the basis and the stimulus for people throughout the organization to find gap-filling solutions. Properly presented gaps can spread excitement and enthusiasm to all levels of a corporation and its divisions or profit centers.

Step 8. What Could We Do? Opportunities/Problems

Act to Fill the Gap

A gap between objectives and business as usual cannot be filled by wishful thinking. It can be filled only by devising, proposing, and approving new strategies and implementing them through new action programs. The emphasis is on the new or different, because we are dealing by definition with directions and achievements beyond business as usual. The gap was created for exactly that purpose.

Do an Opportunity–Problem Feasibility Analysis

You must select major external opportunities and threats facing the business, as well as select your major internal strengths and needs. The emphasis is on *selection*—the strategic determination of the direction to take and the means to be used. Possible action programs should be listed, and priorities must be carefully evaluated.

Since only a few businesses operate under legal monopoly conditions (and a few by illegal oligopoly collusion), competition must be given serious consideration by most enterprises. Competitive strengths and potential moves should be carefully analyzed and kept updated for continuing perspective.

Possible action programs must be further evaluated from two points of view:

1. *Risk-analysis assessment:* Evaluating various components of a program, such as time, costs, need, and impact, to arrive at a relative and judgmental overall rating of success probability

2. *Resource-requirements assessment:* Evaluating various key resource needs, such as people, physical assets, management, and finances, to reach yet another perspective of the relative feasibility and economics of each program

Generate Action Program Proposals

Although most of the possible action program proposals are generated by designated personnel in the formal and continuous planning process, don't disregard another source of innovative proposals. Many companies encourage self-starters anywhere in the organization to organize *ad hoc* task forces and—mostly on their own time—work to prepare and propose what they consider to be worthwhile new endeavors for the corporation. These studies and proposals are not only for new markets, products, or services (revenue-oriented) but also for better internal procedures, efficiency, and savings (cost-oriented). We'll have more to say about task forces later.

Step 9. What Should We Do? Selection of Strategy and Programs

No enterprise has sufficient human, physical, and financial resources to implement all the programs it would like to. At some time in the planning process, it becomes necessary to evaluate, select, and prune. It is an important but also a frustrating task. The final decision is purely judgmental—which is why it must take place at very high, if not the highest, levels of management.

Do a Strategy and Programs Classification

Market position is a key factor in determining future direction. A matrix evaluation of current versus future markets and current versus future products and services should be done very carefully and without emotional bias. This analysis can be used to determine the degree of probable future risk taken by the company, depending on the desired percent of change from the known (current products in current markets) into the unknown (future products in future markets) while taking into account the intermediate steps: current products in future markets and future products in current markets.

The gap fillers—that is, selected new action programs—should be further analyzed by external strategy classification (e.g., horizontal versus vertical expansion) and by internal strategy classification (e.g., marketing versus R&D emphasis).

Make Explicit Commitments

When all the battling, paring, and adjusting have been done, it's time to specifically state the primary and secondary strategies through which the desired objectives are to be achieved. It is also time to establish clear and unequivocal expected financial results, priority of action on the selected programs, and key steps and checkpoint target dates.

Adjust Objectives

We said in step 6 that objectives were to be established emotionally and were to express the true inner hopes and desires of the executives. Now, however, the dreams must be adjusted to cold reality. If the sum total of the new programs—all the gap fillers practically feasible and viable—do not add up to the total gap between the original objectives and the momentum of business as usual, then the objectives must be adjusted and, most likely, reduced to reality. An organization should honestly try to find ways to reach its aspirations; but if it cannot reach them, it must abandon the unrealistic goals. Objectives must be challenging but achievable. Otherwise, the whole process of planning is compromised and may turn into an expensive exercise in futility and frustration.

Step 10. How Can We Do It? Implementation

The planning process does not stop with the general outline of what is to be done. It is a continuous and reiterative process that covers and monitors all phases of management and business activities. Thus, planning is very much concerned with the actual implementation of the new action programs—the gap fillers selected in step 9.

Evaluate the Impact of New Programs

New endeavors generate new relationships, step on a few toes, change established status quos. Analyze the probable impact of implementation of new programs on the traditional "balance of power" between functions, as well as potential changes in direct and indirect business activities. Your goal is to achieve constructive improvement, but you must consider the possibility of temporary disturbance and irritation.

The implementation of every important new program has ramifications throughout the company. It touches, directly or indirectly, on the activities of most other key functions and departments. Try to determine how the addition of gap-filling programs will create changes—both short- and long-range—in functional objectives and operations. Focus on departmental/functional activities in the key areas of marketing, production, R&D, human resources, finance, and administration.

Put greater emphasis on departmental grass roots planning and implementation. The corporate planning process should be aimed at integration and facilitation. Obviously, it should not be performed or perceived as a top-down imposition of bureaucratic procedures, an avalanche of useless paperwork, and a time-consuming piece of drudgery.

Pay particular attention to the potential impact of new and crucial programs on the human side of the enterprise. Be aware that:

- The organization structure may have to be changed.
- A human resources and skills plan must be devised.

- Motivation and incentives should be reexamined.
- Managerial styles could be obsolete and in need of revamping.
- Essential cross-communications patterns should be examined for possible rerouting.

Step 11. How Are We Doing? Control, Control, Control

The last step of gap analysis—or of any planning process—is to monitor progress. Each program proposal must include checkpoints, a timetable, and, of course, budgeted costs. Strict control must be established to assure top management that implementation is proceeding as planned and promised.

Monitor the External Environment

The external environment is not under the company's control. It may often create unpredicted situations which directly affect the key activities of the corporation. A continuous system for monitoring external factors is strongly recommended.

In earlier steps, key external factors and their impact were identified. Objectives, policies, strategies, and programs were devised and selected on the basis of assumptions. This makes it important to be alert to any changes in the external factors and the interpretation of factor impact. Such changes must be analyzed as to their effect on total pertinent market and product and service potentials and the company's market and product and service sales forecasts. This, in turn, may generate key changes in objectives, strategies, and programs. The competitive assessment also may have to be revised.

Analyze Fiscal and Physical Variances

Analyze and deal with potential variances in key areas of the business. Obviously, any one major variance may precipitate a chain reaction throughout the enterprise. The most important final question is whether new and generally more risky programs, instituted because of certain assumptions, are still viable in view of unexpected changes in external factors.

Setting objectives and devising strategies to reach new goals is not expensive. Implementing the strategies through new and additional programs is very expensive. That's where you need well-designed, accurate reporting and fast-acting control, control, control.

Make an Overall Assessment

It is beneficial for management to periodically reexamine the company's progress from a strategic point of view, in addition to reviewing the traditional financial reports. Managers should take stock of their achievements during a predetermined period. What challenges were met? What threats were overcome? What strengths were exploited? What needs were developed? How did all that compare with original objectives? Were the successes major ones? How did they happen? What could be further improved? What changes are necessary?

A good corporate planning process is continuous and reiterative. It strives for constant improvement. It refuses to accept the status quo and battles complacency. It forces managers to deal with greater challenges but makes management fun.

Action proposals: the task force approach

Strategic management must be action-oriented. It is entirely dependent on program proposals: what to do, when to do it, by whom it's to be done, and at what cost. That makes action proposals a vital part of the strategic management process. A central objective of any company should be to stimulate a continuous flow of innovative proposals. One effective way to do that is through task forces. A company can have two kinds of task forces: appointed and voluntary.

Appointed Task Forces

Appointed task forces are company-sponsored, interdisciplinary groups of interested individuals. They are given headings: statements of key issues, problems, or opportunities that management would like to see solved or exploited. Appointed task forces should:

- Have no more than seven participants.
- Be set up for no longer than 3 months.
- Elect their own leaders.
- Have no full-time staff support.

- Report directly to the level able to make a final decision on their proposals.

Voluntary Task Forces

In addition to appointing task forces, a company with an innovative climate can spawn self-generated, voluntary task forces. These are usually started by an intrapreneur with a burning idea and a determination to have it implemented. This champion creates a personal task force composed of individuals sympathetic to his or her cause: ideally, an interdisciplinary team with a great deal of knowledge.

Voluntary task forces should initially conduct business on their own time; otherwise, normal operations would suffer. It can be done by coming to work an hour earlier and leaving an hour later—as well as by taking long lunch breaks. It can add up to a substantial amount of thought and effort over just a few months.

When the team is ready, it seeks an informal review of the proposal with its peers: constructive critiques, reactions, suggestions. The final version is then prepared for presentation to a review board, which should be composed of top executives, including the CEO.

The review board should meet at specified times, and the meetings should never be postponed. Postponements send negative messages to the organization that management is not really serious or enthused about new-programs activity. It kills the intrapreneurial spirit, and everyone retreats to the business-as-usual routine.

If after a presentation the board approves the proposal, obviously everyone is pleased. But a rejection need not kill the intrapreneurial spirit. If the board decides not to accept the proposal but gives a thoughtful explanation for its viewpoint, the team will not get discouraged. It may redo or modify the proposal or start on another self-motivated project. Discouragement sets in when the board makes no decision, procrastinates, and postpones.

The company should also avoid this classic reaction: "The proposal is excellent. It should be implemented, but there is just no money in the budget!" The solution is to create an idea seed fund every year. There should always be a reserve ready to finance new and unbudgeted programs. To give a strong positive signal about its intentions, management should declare that the seed fund is inviolate. That means it will not be reduced, even if all other budgets are cut during the year.

How to Sell an Action Proposal

A task force can come up with excellent ideas for action programs but not know how to sell them to top management. Failure to make an effective presentation can erase months of hard work and painstaking analysis. But creative planners can improve their presentations. Here are some guidelines:

- Any report or plan should be written in a telegraphic style, without prepositions, adjectives, or any unnecessary verbiage. This can make the report 60 percent shorter and more readable.
- Present all items in priority order. There should be no lists, categories, or classifications that are not prioritized.
- Replace descriptive statements with quantified statements whenever possible. Example: "Market share: 1986, 10 percent; 1987, 14 percent," instead of "Our market share next year will be considerably greater due to our very aggressive moves against competition and superior marketing by our highly motivated and better-trained sales force."
- Make conclusions and recommendations crisp and unequivocal. (Harry Truman expressed his dislike of excessive hedging by asking for one-armed economists, so he wouldn't hear "on the one hand it may be this, but on the other hand it may be that.")
- Include a menu of alternatives for strategy and execution. This allows flexibility and gives top management options from which to select.
- At least 10 days before the presentation is scheduled, send management a complete package of facts, data, and supporting material. This gives management a chance to study the proposal in advance. Don't worry about a premature unveiling; most executives won't read it anyhow.

An oral presentation should follow the pyramid approach. Start with what you want to happen, not with a logical sequence that may begin with the history of the company. The span of attention of the typical executive is 12 to 20 minutes, so the key issue must be presented fast. Start out with, "We need a million dollars for automatic haircut machines."

Perhaps the boss will say, "Okay." In that case, stop, fold your charts, and run. Overselling kills more presentations than underselling.

If you don't get an immediate yes, continue your presentation. But present only 20 percent of your knowledge and keep 80 percent back. If you present 100 percent of what you know, the first question will leave you blank. Reserve the 80 percent for additional explanations if necessary.

In describing your program proposal, follow this sequence:

1. Why do we need it?
2. What will it do?
3. How will it be implemented?
4. When will it be completed?
5. Who will do it?
6. How much will it cost?

Visual aids are crucial, but don't use 35-mm slides. The room must be darkened, so you cannot read listeners' expressions. In addition, the sequence of slides is too rigid. A better medium is the overhead projector; it has more flexibility, and the lights can stay on.

It's important to give an oral explanation of the visual aids, but don't quote verbatim what is on the screen. Instead, give pertinent information in addition to what can be read.

Keep the cost of the presentation to a minimum, and don't make the presentation too slick. It should not convey the impression of a con job.

PART FIVE

Winning and Losing Strategies: Twelve Case Studies

Why do we pay attention to case studies? Basically, to derive better insights into what constitutes a winning or losing strategy. What are the key ingredients of successes and messes? How should top management think? What elements should be considered, and how should they be weighed? What's the proper timing for a major shift in strategy and company culture?

CASE STUDY ONE

Eastman Kodak: a powerful giant pays the price for inflexibility.

Here we have the case of Eastman Kodak, perfectly demonstrating what happens when a corporate giant fails to be flexible and adapt to change—and as a result develops a dangerous hardening of the arteries. The company is now struggling hard to regain its prestigious image and rise to its former high performance level. Let's analyze its decline and its efforts to recover.

Anatomy of a Decline (1980–1983)

Over a 10-year period, Kodak's return on equity declined from an outstanding 25 percent to a so-so 7.5 to 10 percent. Net profit margins fell from 18 percent to 8 percent, and discretionary cash flow went from a positive $290 million in 1978 to a negative $446 million in 1983. Here's what accounted for this serious erosion:

1. *Not-invented-here (NIH) syndrome.* Kodak first dismissed the Polaroid instant camera as a passing fad. Later attempts to slice

a share of the market away from Polaroid resulted in losses of $300 million after taxes. The competition ended when Polaroid won its decade-long patent infringement suit in 1986. The issue of a potential $1 billion compensation to Polaroid and to the 16.5 million owners of now-useless Kodak instant cameras had not been resolved at this writing.

2. *Poor new-product development (camera failure).* In 1982, Kodak came out with a disk camera that produced poor pictures. Projected at 14 million units for the year, it sold about 5 million—the photographic Edsel.

3. *Inadequate competitiveness (film failure).* Amateur film is to Kodak what the razor blade is to Gillette. But Kodak allowed itself to be beaten to the punch by Fuji, which came out with 400 ASA film 6 months before the American company got its own version on the market. Fuji is still the only company that makes 16000 ASA high-speed film. You can't minimize foreign competition, especially when it's Japanese.

4. *"Arrogance."* Kodak lost the 1986 Olympic games sponsorship—which was invaluable advertising—because, according to Olympic chairman Peter Ueberroth, "They were so arrogant...."

5. *Overly cautious diversification (copiers).* Kodak first scorned Xerox (again, NIH) and then spent tons of money to enter the market in 1975. It had an excellent product, but it failed to market aggressively and has lost share since 1981. Even IBM, a late entry in 1982, overtook Kodak, which is now down to 18 percent market share from a high of 50 percent in 1981.

6. *Unsuccessful diversification (blood analyzers).* DuPont got into blood analyzers in 1971, and Kodak's 1981 entry (14 years in development) was too late. After a long-term 15 percent growth, the market is now flat. According to the DuPont Diagnostic Systems Division, Kodak's $600 million investment is dead.

7. *Unsuccessful acquisitions.* Kodak purchased Mead's ink-jet printer division so it could develop nonimpact printers, but at the time of this writing it hadn't come out with a product. Kodak also acquired Atex, a leading maker of electronic text processing equipment. But Atex has been slashing prices and losing market share

since then. After Atex lost its No. 1 position in the market, Kodak installed a third new management team to try to pull the ailing acquisition out of its slump.

8. *Loss of quality service.* "Processed by Kodak" used to stand for the highest quality of film processing—the company's historic stronghold. No more. Kodak began to cut corners and service became sloppy, which opened the door to independent processing stores and mail-order processors.

Kodak Tries a Turnaround—But Will It Work?

Kodak management finally started to react to its decline late in 1983. It took the following steps:

1. *Personnel layoffs and dismissals.* Kodak ended its historic lifetime employment policy. It first let go 11,000 employees, 8 percent of its work force. Combined with a wage freeze, the reduction did nothing to help morale. Nor did the fact that 12,800 more employees were slated for dismissal in 1986. Budget cuts, write-offs, and other unusual pretax charges against profits amounted to $563 million in 1985 and $708 million in 1986.

2. *Reorganization into business units.* Kodak's photographic business—representing 80 percent of total sales—was split into 17 units organized by product. Some attempt was made to decentralize decision making. New managers and consultants were brought in from outside. (In contrast, only one person, a general counsel, had been brought into top management from the outside during the preceding 30 years.)

3. *Marketing others' products.* For the first time in its history, Kodak will sell other manufacturers' goods under its own name: Matsushita's 8-mm videocassette camera, Canon's medium-volume copier, Dysan's floppy disk, and TDK's videotape. But, as was pointed out earlier in this book, unless Kodak adds genuine value in its resale to the customer, simply sticking its labels on those products won't pay off.

4. *Manufacturing for others.* For the first time, Kodak will manufacture products for resale under different brand names.

5. *New communication venture.* Kodak has set up Eastman Communications to compete with AT&T, IBM, MCI, and GTE in information technology. (Seems like an overambitious entry into an unfamiliar field dominated by giants.)

6. *New-product development.* Kodak managed to get its dry battery on the market only 2 years after the concept was originated. It also introduced two 35-mm cameras to counteract the Japanese invasion. Kodak's "disposable" camera is new, but it's a me-too copy of the original Fuji version.

Kodak is trying to recover, but there's a serious flaw in its efforts. The problem is at the top. New markets, new technologies, and new, powerful competition require far greater boldness than Kodak's top management has demonstrated thus far. In my view, it's doubtful that the company can regain its lost edge under the leadership of Chairman Colby Chandler (34 years at Kodak) and President Kay Whitmore (27-year veteran). We'll see.

Lesson to Be Learned

Kodak's problems reflect the lack of adaptability to change, particularly in product development. Its case is not unique by any means. Some of the most successful giants of the past do not understand the new structural need for faster product development. Three forces contribute to this requirement: (1) faster changing technology (only 3 to 4 years between breakthroughs) (2) stronger global competition, and (3) faster market saturation (massive distribution).

The results of Kodak's slowness clearly demonstrate that serial, methodical, step-by-step product development must be replaced by more complex and risky parallel development to compress the time for introducing new products. Matsushita, Casio, and Coca-Cola have learned how, while P&G and Sony are struggling with the problem. One potential solution: Vertically integrated joint ventures to create "instant" new products and to take advantage of the diverse strengths of the various partners in such areas as marketing, distribution, manufacturing, and R&D.

CASE STUDY TWO

Hasbro: From "hasbeen" to No. 1 toy maker

Eight years ago, Hasbro was called "Hasbeen" because of its huge losses. Now it's the No. 1 toy maker in the world with $1.2 billion in sales, $99 million in profits, and the third-best 5-year ROI of the 1000 largest companies. Good performance in a very fickle business is an unusual phenomenon. Hasbro's success is due to a determined strategy aggressively executed:

1. *Product philosophy.* Toys must offer lasting play value, ability to be shared, and ability to stimulate the imagination.

2. *Product strategy.* Develop a major toy with staying power and keep supplying new add-ons—the systems approach. Example: a $100 aircraft carrier plus extension through a steady stream of "allowance money" planes, hovercraft, action figures, and so on.

3. *Advertising.* Continually rekindle interest. Hasbro produces its own Saturday morning TV cartoons featuring its toys. They're really full-length commercials.

4. *Market growth.* Provide product availability from cradle to adulthood—toys and games for all ages.

5. *Product development.* Ideas can come from anywhere; idea people are not separated from development people. Products originate internally, are bought from the outside, or are copied from the competition—whatever is necessary.

6. *Management style.* Mixture of solid management practices and intuition. Example: combining scientific market research with seat-of-the-pants hunches.

Hasbro has its critics. They point to product failures, copycat tactics, excessive number of gut feeling decisions, arrogance, opportunism, lack of trend setting. Maybe so, but Hasbro must be doing something right to have sharply increased its profits and passed Mattel as No. 1 toy maker.

Lesson to Be Learned

Time will tell if Hasbro's specific strategies will still be valid tomorrow. But the company is clearly demonstrating three vital attributes that any business must have to succeed today: clear market focus, precise direction, and action orientation.

CASE STUDY THREE

Toys "R" Us: Implementing three simple principles pays off big.

Retailer Toys "R" Us is expected to pass 20 percent market share in 1988, up from 12 percent in 1983. Revenues for 1988 are projected at $3.7 billion, up from $1.3 billion in 1983, with net income keeping pace with these spectacular increases.

The chain has 233 warehouse-style, self-service stores that average 45,000 square feet and are filled with 18,000 discounted items. Each store is deliberately located away from shopping centers to attract "full attention and intention" customers. This tactic pays off in bigger sales per customer.

A brainchild of Charles P. Lazarus, the firm follows precise, innovative policies and is imbued with a "fanatical dedication" to a few key principles. The mega-strategy is: Offer customers *selection*, *stock*, and *price*.

1. *Selection principle.* Toys "R" Us provides choice by stocking a great variety of similar items—e.g., 35 different strollers, 12 different cribs. Items include not only the latest popular toys but also staples like construction paper, party hats, and birthday candles; Lazarus calls them the bread-and-butter items. Another clever

strategy is to stock baby products, such as disposable diapers and carriages, at low prices. This attracts mothers with babies and can tie the growing family to Toys "R" Us for the next 12 to 15 years.

2. *Stock principle.* All items sold must be readily available on the floor to inspect, purchase, and carry out. Sophisticated computer tracking of each item helps keep inventory moving and spots hot items before the competition does.

3. *Price principle.* All items are discounted and priced competitively. But high-demand winners like Cabbage Patch dolls are discounted even deeper and sold at minimal profit. This astute policy creates an overall image of offering the lowest bargain prices for *all* items. Toys "R" Us managers understand that excessive greed on one hot item can alienate the customer forever. The chain sticks to its price principle so faithfully that it reverses the usual procedure of purchasing items at wholesale and then setting the retail price. Instead, it sets the optimum retail price first and then negotiates a wholesale price to match it.

Objective: More Growth

Lazarus is still the dominant figure and innovator, but Toys "R" Us is no longer a one-man show. He has built loyalty and assembled a young, hungry, aggressive management team to keep the business growing and evolving. Nevertheless, he maintains a close watch on operations. He may exasperate some of his managers by tracking daily store sales on his computer terminal in his vacation home, but he makes a point: the importance of control, control, control.

The company is still expanding and also diversifying. Going international, it already has 14 stores in Canada, Singapore, and Britain. Objective: to move gradually to become the largest toy chain in the world. This has been accompanied by a diversification into clothing through Kids "R" Us stores. So far there are 23 outlets, and plans are to multiply at the conservative rate of 20 per year.

Lesson to Be Learned

Toys "R" Us shows clearly how success can be achieved by innovatively implementing a few guiding principles. The principles don't have to be original. After all, what's new about trying to attract and hold customers by offering a large selection of goods at low prices? The key to success here was the action orientation, the fresh implementation of generalities. That is what made Toys "R" Us one of the most outstanding business-growth case studies in recent years. Just one example of the constant flow of new marketing ideas: In 1987, Toys "R" Us announced major price reductions in line with savings to be achieved through the new tax code.

Advice: Whatever business you are in, establish a few guiding principles and implement them extremely well—without compromises, without exceptions, without deviations. You'll do better with simplicity than complexity.

CASE STUDY FOUR

IBM: Learning that nothing is forever

IBM has been super successful for over 70 years. It has lived up to the principles of its founder, Thomas J. Watson, Sr.: respect for the individual, pursuit of excellence, great customer service, and in-depth employee training. There were no hidden or complex secrets to IBM's continuous success. Any organization that could and would hire bright and highly motivated people, train them well, reward them generously, and imbue them with the single goal of satisfying the customer would rapidly master the IBM "secret."

IBM was always first on my list of best-managed companies worldwide. I may be biased. I still refer to IBM as "we" even though I left it in 1965, when sales were $3.5 billion vs. $50 billion today. The Big Blue culture and integrity created for decades the leading example of management excellence and highly profitable supergrowth. But nothing is forever.

A Giant with Giant Problems

The electronic revolution dramatically changed the price/performance ratio of computing devices. As new micros replace minis and minis challenge expensive mainframes, a huge price war is building. A conservative present estimate is 4:1—a $3000 IBM PC-XT could be replaced by a $750 Hyundai clone; a $350,000 DEC superminicomputer could be replaced by a $75,000 Sun workstation; a $900,000 mainframe could be replaced by a $100,000 network of 32-bit microcomputers with additional savings of over $300,000 a year in software fees, programming costs, and maintenance contracts.

All that represents a great opportunity and fast growth potential for start-up companies with no inventory or sales record to protect. But for IBM, with $35 billion tied up in obsolete, overpriced hardware, it's a nightmare. The hardware amounts to 70 percent of IBM's yearly sales.

The time frame is short. By 1990, the 32-bit minicomputers, networks, and superior software will become the mainstream of the data processing market. In 1987, IBM's challenge was to sell 4 times as many MIPS (million instructions per second) in the next 3 years just to stay even. And that did not include an additional exposure to $5 billion in losses of software and maintenance contracts.

What IBM Has to Do

In early 1987, IBM announced a new family of personal computers. But that was not a viable solution to the company's long-term problems. The new products were far from satisfying the new market demand. Again, it was too little, too late. It will take revolutionary, not evolutionary, steps to create a new momentum. IBM will have to appoint a hatchetman to clean house, reduce costs, innovate and pioneer, change its reliance on obsolete strategies, and move again. Here are some actions it must take:

1. *Change R&D philosophy and direction.* IBM is still hooked on mainframe technology and is trying to protect the past. It's behind on networking, compatibility, new software, and the 32-bit Intel 80386 chip. IBM spends $4.7 billion on R&D and engineering, more than the total revenue of some of its key competitors. But it's time for it to shake up and redirect its efforts or buy innovation on the outside—which may be faster and cheaper.

2. *Change manufacturing and procurement strategy.* If South Korean clones can be sold for one-quarter of IBM's price and with 4 times its warranty length, a major restructuring of production and procurement is a must. IBM is proud of its 100,000 suppliers worldwide—but that's far too many. Modern, just-in-time practices require drastic consolidation and reduction of the number of vendors.

3. *Change marketing techniques.* IBM strength was always in selling large companies through top contacts. Big Blue never understood small business or knew how to deal with "little people" and today's increasingly independent divisions and departments of large organizations. Decentralized operations require supportive, knowledgeable, local hand-holding. IBM must learn that service means providing business solutions, not hardware maintenance.

4. *Change the cost structure.* That's the toughest job. Previous steps require reallocation of resources. But IBM also needs major cost reductions, massive cutting of expenses. Large, successful organizations grow fat and complacent and need periodic shakeouts. Asking 4000 employees to consider early retirement or transferring 5000 to the field sales force is a drop in the bucket for a company with 405,000 employees. By 1990, IBM must release at least 50,000 employees—even if that means abandoning the full-employment policy it has maintained so faithfully for 50 years.

Lesson to Be Learned

When the world changes but you and your business don't change, it's a surefire prescription for trouble. No matter how successful it has been in the past, a corporation cannot rely on its prestige, its previous triumphs, and its traditional way of doing things for future success. Instead, it must take a realistic look at the world as it is, not as it was, and adapt to that world with fresh strategies, faster decisions, more flexibility, and action-oriented implementation.

CASE STUDY FIVE

Beatrice: Presiding over disaster

When, in 1986, the directors of Beatrice Company took the long overdue step of replacing Chairman James L. Dutt, the events leading to Dutt's downfall were reported in great detail by *Fortune, Business Week,* and *The Wall Street Journal.* Here is a brief summary of their reports:

Beatrice became a $13.5 billion giant by acquiring Esmark ($2.7 billion) in 1984. The price was too high; it resulted in immense long-term debt. The debt soared from 38 percent to 108 percent of equity, and the annual interest of $382 million was 50 percent higher than the company's total net earnings. Why did Beatrice, valued at 6 times earnings, pay 23 times earnings for Esmark? The answer is Dutt's lofty but misdirected vision of becoming the "premier worldwide marketer."

From the time Esmark was acquired, it was all downhill for Beatrice. The following factors were among those responsible:

1. *Executive turnover.* In 5 years under Dutt, over 40 of 58 top executives, including the COO (who was never replaced), quit or were fired. The La Choy foods and Tropicana juice divisions

each saw three presidents come and go in rapid succession. Heads of the best Esmark executives rolled immediately after the takeover. (Critics, inside and outside the organization, report that Dutt was intolerant of dissent or debate and that his repeated firing threats helped demoralize talented top executives.)

2. *Marketing strategy.* A costly, overkill national TV ad campaign was launched to make Beatrice a household name. Commercials during the 1986 Olympics alone cost $30 million. The overall marketing budget was raised from $160 million to $800 million! The attempt to link together Tropicana orange juice, Samsonsite luggage, Peter Pan peanut butter, Playtex underwear, Waterloo toolboxes, and Kreip corned beef into one positive consumer image bordered on the ridiculous. And the $70 million commitment to an auto-racing sponsorship, with no direct connection to any Beatrice product, was sheer corporate insanity.

3. *Rubber-stamp board.* Board members—12 out of 18 of whom were appointed by Dutt—waited far too long to question the disastrous strategy of the CEO they paid $1.2 million a year. During his 5-year tenure, the return on equity and earnings per share decreased, interest soared, and Beatrice's securities ratings were downgraded. Beatrice became bigger but less profitable, less viable, and far riskier. The company's long-term future was in jeopardy. Finally, the board brought in two retired Beatrice executives to pick up the pieces. But apparently, the job of rebuilding morale, correcting the excess, and making the company sound again was just too much. Kohlberg, Kravis, Roberts & Company organized a leveraged buy-out and took Beatrice private—with the objective of short-term financial gains, not long-range economic growth. Almost immediately, the principals began dismantling Beatrice by selling its most profitable and exciting businesses, such as its huge soft drink bottling complex. It looks as though there will not be much left of the company a few years from now.

Lesson to Be Learned

In the past, many successful companies have been run as one-man shows by corporate czars: Ford, Sr. at Ford, Watson, Sr. at IBM, Sarnoff at RCA, Geneen at ITT. But it doesn't work anymore.

Times have changed. To manage a large or even a small organization today requires a genuine team effort. Talented top executives no longer want to work as docile puppets, even at high pay. Among many other companies, Continental Illinois, Eastern, Gulf & Western, and Control Data are trying to shed one-man rule and repair the serious damage it did to their long-term future.

Advice: Analyze your own management style—objectively. If you detect even the faintest trace of destructive behavior, make a commitment to yourself and to your organization to change fast. And if you happen to report to a destructive boss, start planning your escape now, before you lose your self-respect, peace of mind, and any satisfaction in your work.

CASE STUDY SIX

Sakowitz and Commodore: Victims of a fast-changing world

What do Sakowitz, Inc. and Commodore International, Ltd. have in common? One is an 83-year-old high-fashion specialty store chain; the other is a high-tech computer company. But both have tumbled rapidly from heights of success to financial ruin: Sakowitz is in Chapter 11, and in a single quarter of 1985, Commodore reported a $124 million loss with sales 55 percent off the corresponding period. Reason: Overambitious plans and expectations by top management in an unpredictable economic world.

Sakowitz

Bobby Sakowitz (Harvard graduate, fourth-generation chairman) summarized the situation accurately: "Nothing exceeds like excess." Sakowitz launched an expansion program in oil-rich Texas; it doubled its number of stores and grew at a double-digit rate when the rest of retailing was in a slump. But temporary success hid fundamental strategic errors:

1. *Excessive leveraging:* tripling debt for store expansion, stocking a highly volatile fashion inventory, and buying back family stock
2. *One-man show:* doing everything himself, from buying to merchandising, from store remodeling to minute office details
3. *Part-time attention to business:* too many extracurricular activities such as a bank chairmanship, an airline directorship, a consultantship to Joseph Magnin Company (also in Chapter 11), time-consuming civic activities, and too-frequent worldwide traveling
4. *Panic solutions to the oil bust:* markdowns, discounting, more advertising, new inventories, "buying time" until the return of the oil boom—which didn't happen.

Commodore

Commodore was a profitable supergrowth company with $1.3 billion in sales for fiscal 1984. It projected $5 billion goals for the future. But then the home-computer market collapsed, leaving Commodore with $300 to $400 million in obsolete inventory. As with Sakowitz, Commodore's dizzying rise hid fundamental strategic errors:

1. *Inventory.* Excessive inventory, based on failure to recognize fast technological changes and even faster changes in consumer buying patterns.

2. *Management.* An ill-timed, major change in top management style. Jack Tramiel, whose style can be described as both autocratic and flamboyant, was replaced by conservative, analytical, deliberate Marshall Smith. But the timing was atrocious. You don't make long-range plans for better swamp drainage when you're up to your ears in alligators.

3. *Marketing.* As with Sakowitz, poorly chosen strategies to keep sales high: markdowns, discounting, new-product promises, more advertising, "buying time" until the slump in home computers ended (it never did).

Now Commodore is betting the company on essentially one new

product: the Amiga computer. But this $1800 high-priced home computer and low-priced business computer is positioned in the worst possible spot: between the consumer's lack of money for an expensive toy and the business buyer's lack of confidence in a "cheap" computer. Only time will tell if the gamble will pay off, but I'm not betting on it.

Lesson to Be Learned

The same thing that happened to Sakowitz and Commodore can happen to any business that—like high-fashion retailing and high-tech computers—is extremely volatile because of changing economic conditions, changing fads, and increased competition among giants. (When Neiman-Marcus fights Marshall Field and IBM fights Apple, Sakowitz and Commodore lose.)

Advice: Don't push your business to extremes. You are faced with present and future eras of high fluctuations, faster changes in market demand, shorter product and service life cycles, greater competition, and rapid technological obsolescence. These conditions require:

- Deliberately controlled growth and profit management
- A lower overall break-even point—at least 20 percent lower
- Lower, not higher, debt leverage
- Ruthless amputation when a product or market begins to evaporate (don't throw good money after bad)
- Participative management in good times, authoritarian style in crisis—not vice versa

CASE STUDY SEVEN

People Express: Crash landing for a high flyer

Don Burr formed People Express in 1981; he was betting on deregulation. His strategy had these elements:

- Make it possible for customers to fly where and when they want at prices they like.
- Hurt the biggies by enticing passengers through low fares.
- Make a profit by buying and leasing secondhand airplanes.
- Motivate nonunion employees with share ownership.
- Run a lean, no-frills, flexible organization.

The result: huge success. The People Express story was told and taught as a shining example of modern entrepreneurship and innovative management. In 5 years, People grew from three Boeings and a small group of dedicated "owners" to 78 aircraft and 3402 full-time employees. From 1 million passengers at nondescript eastern airports, People eventually handled 12 million passengers through a network spanning Vancouver, Los Angeles, London, and Brussels. People stock zoomed from $5 to $24.

The Biggies Declare War

Big established airlines tolerated People when it was small, but they declared war when Donald Burr tried to move out of his niche market onto their turf. They used their sophisticated computer reservation systems to match or beat People's fares on just enough of their seats (with full service) to lure away enough of People's passengers to reduce its load factor below the 65 percent break-even point. People was flying at 75 percent load factor in 1983 and 67 percent in early 1986. By late 1986, it had plummeted far below 50 percent.

At that point I wrote in the September 1986 issue of my publication, *Kami Strategic Assumptions:*

> The future of People Express is bleak. Stock is at $4 after refusing an $8 per share offer by Texas Air. The plans are to change from no-frills to full-service (me-too) operations. If that's the innovative solution to People Express problems and Mr. Burr's competitive strategy with American and United, it will not be around for the Christmas rush.

It was not. Shortly afterward, People Express was acquired by Texas Air, which folded it into Continental Airlines.

How to Turn Triumph into Disaster

The demise of People Express can be blamed on several fundamental errors:

1. *Frontal attack on biggies.* You don't take on giants with pockets much deeper than yours; they can stand the losses far longer than you can.

2. *Deteriorating service.* When People was small and friendly, it was fun; when it overexpanded, it became known as "People Distress." It had a 10.4 FAA complaint ratio vs. 4.9 at Pan Am, 3.0 at Eastern, and 0.6 at Delta.

3. *Rising costs.* Other airlines drastically reduced their operating costs with lower union agreements, two-tier hiring, and more

economical new equipment—while "lean" People became sloppy (higher pilot and attendant starting rates than at United or TWA).

4. *Lack of sophisticated tools.* You can't compete without an extensive computer network for reservations, fare and discount calculation, and fast, competitive retaliation.

5. *Disastrous 1985 acquisition of Frontier Airlines.* People paid $307 million for a full-service airline with 44 aircraft and 4800 unionized employees. It didn't make sense. Burr changed Frontier to no-frills, started a fare war, and lost thousands of customers. Within 9 months of its acquisition, Frontier was a bankrupt shell.

Lesson to Be Learned

People Express enjoyed 3 years of success based on entrepreneurship, motivation, a brilliant degree of uniqueness, focused strategy, enthusiastic implementation. But it all went down the drain because of the strategic errors cited above. Every manager will say: "How could this really have happened? The mistakes were so classic, so obvious, so inane." Were they? Yes! Could it happen to your company? Yes! Don't let it.

CASE STUDY EIGHT

Harley-Davidson: Revving up for a fast turnaround

More than 100 U.S. companies once made motorcycles. Since 1954, there has been only one: Harley-Davidson, founded in 1903. Harley's fortunes varied over the years, but its legend grew. AMF acquired the company in 1969 and sold it in 1981 to 13 Harley executives, who assumed an $80.5 million debt.

Sputtering toward Disaster

Immediately, everything that could go wrong, did. The new entrepreneurial Harley-Davidson company was caught in a Honda-Yamaha discount war. Its market share went from 17 to 12.5 percent; a deep recession eroded sales and production; morale plunged; and the company lost $30 million in 1981–1982.

Outsiders predicted imminent bankruptcy. They were wrong. Knowing there was little time left, the new owners acted swiftly and decisively. They defined their niche market: classic, heavyweight motorcycles. They defined their goal: to successfully compete with Japanese giants.

They defined their priorities:

1. To reduce the break-even point from 50,000 to 30,000 units
2. To reduce unit costs
3. To step up quality improvement programs begun in the 1970s
4. To increase market share

Gearing Up for Recovery

After studying Japanese manufacturing techniques, Harley executives extracted the concepts that could be adapted to the U.S. workplace. Some radical changes were made:

- Harley developed an efficient blend of employee participation in a sophisticated production system.
- The organizational structure was streamlined and flattened.
- The company was divided into miniplants.
- Staff jobs were cut; quality control as a separate staff function was eliminated.
- Managers assumed responsibility for quality, production control, manufacturing, industrial engineering, and—sometimes—purchasing.
- Operators assumed line responsibility for production, quality, and even repairs of their own machinery.
- A majority of employees were given 30 to 40 hours of classroom training in statistical process control so they could sample and analyze data on the job.
- Half the employees were organized into quality circles (QCs).
- A common problem-solving "language" was developed among the various departments.
- An overall materials-as-needed (MAN) program, based on just-in-time principles, was developed for both Harley units and their suppliers.
- The number of vendors was reduced by 48 percent. The main criterion for retaining vendors was willingness to adopt just-in-time, apply statistical process control techniques, and involve em-

ployees in their own manufacturing operations. Selected vendors were trained in those techniques by Harley personnel.

Back in the Black

The results of Harley's turnaround efforts are impressive. Consider the progress achieved since 1981 in these areas:

Productivity improvement	+ 45%
Inventories reduction	− 61%
Scrap and rework	− 68%
Defect-free motorcycles	+ 46%
Warranty costs per motorcycle	− 36%
Work force reduction	− 47%
Grievances per employee	− 20%
Absenteeism per employee	− 55%

Moreover, when the 1977–1981 period is compared with the 1981–1985 period, recalls per year went down 67 percent and motorcycles recalled per 1000 produced dropped 85 percent.

Harley's motorcycle business is back in the black, with sales approaching the $300 million mark. In 1986, some 36,700 "hogs" were manufactured in the United States and sold worldwide. The company has regained market position (19.4 percent share in 1986) and is steadily pursuing a program of diversification to broaden its revenue base.

Lesson to Be Learned

A company can turn its fortunes around, even with limited financial resources. It takes, first, tremendous energy and dedication from the management team. The Harley case shows what can be done when there is vision, creativity, and determination. It also shows that break-even can be sharply reduced by reducing the workforce, training and motivating workers, computerizing communications, automating, flattening the organization, and installing new, more efficient methods.

CASE STUDY NINE

Sony: A premium-price innovator is plagued by low-price imitators.

Sony was a proud, global pioneer, a paragon of quality, innovation, and supergrowth—and the most cited example of Japanese-style management success.

No longer. In 1986, Sony—which used to be No. 1—was not even *on* the annual list of the 50 best-managed companies in Japan. It is afflicted with static growth, tumbling profits, loss of market share, burdensome long-term debt, major lifetime-employment problems, and obsolete plants and machinery.

What happened? The answer can be found in four basic problem areas:

1. *Loss of premium-price advantage.* Sony must charge premium prices for its innovative products because the cost of technological leadership is high (it's called the pioneer's tax). Sony's R&D costs are 8 to 10 percent of sales vs. competitors' 4 to 5 percent. This differential was economically feasible when Sony's innovative advantage lasted from 2 to 3 years. Now imitators are on the market in 4 to 8 months with similar high-quality products at prices 20

to 40 percent lower than Sony's. When customers refuse to pay premium prices, sales growth flattens and profits drop.

2. *Loss of market share.* It is not enough to innovate; you must maintain your initial advantage. Sony pioneered the VCR market with Betamax in 1975. By 1983, with 13 competitors selling VCRs at lower prices, Sony's 100 percent market share had eroded to 14 percent.

3. *High production costs.* Like many innovation-driven organizations, Sony neglected cost controls. Surprisingly, it suffers from high labor content and lack of automation. The ratios of sales per employee are revealing: Sony, $104,600; Matsushita (Sony's biggest rival), $122,600; Sharp, $143,000; Sanyo (highly automated), $187,300. Sony's questionable international strategy was to open plants in the United States and Europe—close to market but with higher labor costs. By contrast, Matsushita and Sanyo use Mexico, Taiwan, and Malaysia.

4. *Obsolete leadership.* Sony Chairman Akio Morita is a personal hero of mine: a statesman, an innovator, a philosopher, a legend, and the prime mover of Sony's past success. Unfortunately, he is out of step with the new business environment. It is his operating president, Norio Ogha, who is trying to change the company in response to new conditions. He is instituting cost controls and profit centers, discontinuing obsolete operations, and reorganizing the company structure. Sony will recover, but the recovery will be a long and difficult process.

Lesson to Be Learned

Faster, timelier reaction to new conditions is essential. Sony must change from an innovation-driven to a market-driven organization, from a freewheeling to a cost-conscious business. It must change leadership philosophy—and leaders, if necessary. It must automate and modernize to compete effectively worldwide.

Complacency and business myopia are the two most dangerous diseases of business. Sony's troubles show us that managers must periodically evaluate their company's culture, policies, and strategies—objectively and critically. In today's era of faster change, management must be willing to react faster with often drastic departures from the policies and practices of the past. The legendary Sony waited too long. It will come back, but its mystique of uniqueness and invulnerability is gone.

CASE STUDY TEN

Procter & Gamble: A faltering giant changes its ways.

For decades, P&G was the undisputed leader in consumer products and the role model for competitors in growth, profitability, quality, new-product introduction, and uncanny skill in marketing and market research.

But the giant ran into serious trouble during the mid-1980s because competition became more aggressive and successfully introduced many new and improved products. P&G management was caught napping and did not adapt rapidly enough to changing conditions. During those years, the company lost market share and/or profitability in many major product categories. Competitors narrowed the quality and reputation gap, increased their marketing efficiency, and eroded P&G profits through price cutting.

P&G did not just falter in single skirmishes. It began to lose the war in detergents, fabric softeners, toothpaste, and diapers. Its introduction of soft drinks and orange juice was slower and much costlier than anticipated.

Profits declined in 1985 for the first time in 33 years as reawakening P&G invested heavily in new brands and improvements to existing products.

Discarding the Old "Winning" Ways

After too long a period of inertia, P&G is now vigorously fighting back to stem the erosion and reverse its decline. New strategies are being established and implemented. Old "winning" ways are now being discarded:

Old strategies and policies	New strategies and policies
Slow, serial introduction of new products.	Parallel introduction of four or more big products. High investment.
Long, detailed, meticulous market research and geographical tests.	Shorter, riskier market tests. Faster national introduction and advertising.
Concentration on brand-new products. Strategy of innovation. Disdain of me-too tactics.	Line extensions (Liquid Tide), "flankers" (Ivory shampoo), "flavors" (lemon and pine scents for Cascade and Spic & Span).
Premium-price, premium-quality products only. No cheapies.	Penetration of low-priced market with bargain brands (e.g., cheap toilet paper: Banner).
Laissez-faire or standback attitude (some critics call it "arrogance") with wholesalers and retailers.	Cooperation with distributors, higher built-in margins for retailers. P&G now listens (e.g., it changed Ivory bottles and Tide powder boxes to save space and handling).
Concentration on supermarkets.	Wooing of drugstore chains for personal-care products distribution.
Reliance on volume to hold down unit costs.	Insistence on lowest-cost production for each product. High investment for cost saving, automation, robots (30 percent of capital budget).
Adherence to hierarchical, pyramid-style, methodical, very documented, sequential decision-making management processes.	New business teams, task forces for faster product introduction. Cross-level participation of personnel for cost reduction or new programs. Greater dissemination of previously restricted information.

The new winning ways turned the company around. P&G regained in 2 years most of its product losses and market share, despite the doom and gloom predictions—or hopes—of the competition and some stock analysts. By the end of 1986, sales and profits were growing at a very respectable rate: Sales were up 15 percent to $16 billion, while profits were up 12 percent to $700 million.

Lesson to Be Learned

P&G learned a lesson and did something about it. Today's competition is stronger and will continue to be so. It no longer imitates P&G (although it is often staffed by P&G alumni). Now the competition pioneers and innovates, and P&G—150 years old in 1987—must do the same things to keep up with the times. Today's consumers are sophisticated and fickle. They must be satisfied fast or they will instantly switch brands, leaving brand loyalty in the dust.

Advice: Examine P&G's before-and-after strategies and policies. Compare them with your own company's situation. Are there any similarities, any lessons? Any food for thought? If so, do something about it next Monday morning.

CASE STUDY ELEVEN

Federal Express: Using advanced technology to win big

Started in 1972, Federal Express is the only company ever to hit $1 billion in sales before the end of its first decade of existence. Its success is based on two factors:

1. *Innovative use of the hub-and-spoke distribution system.* Over 500,000 packages are flown nightly into the Memphis airport from all over the United States—and then air-freighted back to their ultimate destinations on 72 planes owned by Federal Express. Although the hub concept had been used for years by airlines for passenger traffic, it took Federal Express founder Fred Smith to recognize that it could work for package delivery as well. As was mentioned in an earlier chapter of this book, his idea met with almost universal ridicule—until he proved he was right.

2. *Extensive use of data processing and communications technology.* Federal Express uses 20,000 terminals for communications between its 40,000 employees and its customers. Many have direct tie-ins. At the peak hours of 2:00 PM to 4:00 PM, some 125,000 customer calls must be handled—that's 17 per second. (Federal Express has no fear of electronics equipment; its 10 top

customers are electronics manufacturers in need of fast distribution, although IBM recently gave all its business to Airborne.)

The key to this very complex system is *connectivity:* the ability to access a huge common database and cross-communicate data wherever needed, in real time. Over 400 dispatch stations communicate via satellite to 15,000 moving delivery vans and to foot couriers equipped with special hand-held processors. The company can almost instantly locate shipping documents and trace package status anywhere from pickup to delivery.

This extensive use of electronic technology is not cheap. Federal Express allocates 6 percent of its revenue to it—a high ratio by conventional business standards. But it's a small price to pay when the entire business depends on data processing performance. Federal Express professes an intense determination to integrate all facets of the business electronically and is doing it well.

Fred Smith's philosophy is deceptively simple: "People/Service/Profit." Hire, train, and motivate good people; that, in turn, will give the customer good service and bring in profits. It is also implicit that dedicated employees must be supported by the latest available technology.

Will Success Spoil Federal Express?

Fred Smith started to redefine his business by shifting into telecommunications, but his first major move in that direction was a failure: He bet and lost some $500 million on ZapMail, an electronic mail system that flopped resoundingly and reduced company profits for at least 2 years.

The latest shock wave is a potential industrywide price war. As of 1987, Federal Express enjoyed a 53 percent market share ($3.2 billion revenue) of the overnight delivery business. Its nearest competitor was United Parcel Service, with 13 percent market share ($800 million revenue). But UPS has the advantage of being a huge organization. With its 84,000 land vehicles and 95 jets (with 20 more on order) it makes 12 times as many deliveries as Federal. A monumental battle is shaping up as customers become more cost-conscious and the market begins to saturate. The first losers will be the smallies, like Purolator Courier. Then the battle for market share will start nipping at the profit margins of the biggies. I still bet on Federal Express. It has class!

Lesson to Be Learned

Federal Express provides an excellent model for other businesses to follow. Every business—big or small—must wholeheartedly adapt to the new era of knowledge, information, and communication. The adaptation starts at the top: Chief executives and top management should be thoroughly familiar and at ease with electronics, computers, robotics, terminals, databases, and transmission facilities. Their example will permeate through the organization and create the new information culture essential to business success in today's environment.

Business decisions today must be made three times as fast as in the past, but without additional risk. You can achieve that if pertinent data are available twice as fast, communicated twice as fast, and analyzed three times as fast. But to realize that, you must be totally committed to:

- Providing and using the latest available technology to improve your databases, data processing, and communications.
- Organizing all your operating units to take advantage of the new technology (e.g., decentralization, fewer reporting layers, and intrapreneurial culture, closer to the action).
- Upgrading your high-talent pool. Don't provide dummies with faster tools. They'll make twice as many mistakes.

CASE STUDY TWELVE

H-C Industries: How to bet your company— and win

Here's the rags-to-riches story of a small, private company. Its uniqueness is a rare blend of innovative, "swinging" entrepreneurship and professional management strategies and execution.

The "Rags" Years

When Robert Smith found himself jobless in Crawfordsville, Indiana, he started developing, building, and overhauling machines to manufacture a tinplate bottle cap and the cork liner for sealing it tightly on beer bottles. He had so little money that he built most of the equipment from materials he found in local scrap and salvage yards. His entire family—including his young son Jim, who was already helping him in "production"—lived in one room. The first orders for bottle caps—today called crowns—were delivered by a friendly police officer because Smith's had no phone.

Progress was slow; over the next 10 years, the business grew to only $210,000. Then disaster struck in 1940, when the entire plant was destroyed by fire. While insurance, a second mortgage, and a supportive local community rebuilt the facility, a friendly competitor volunteered to produce orders for Smith's customers to save the company from going out of business! Smith's even made a profit that year: $177.40.

Overcoming major obstacles during the following years, the small company diversified into the soft drink market. Then founder Robert Smith suffered a series of debilitating heart attacks; he died in 1955. His son Jim, fresh out of college, was thrown into ownership and management. Fortunately, his father had been foresighted enough to establish a strong, experienced board of directors, which proved to be of great help to the young new leader.

Necessity is Still the Mother of Invention

The tiny company based its management strategy on three strong beliefs:

- That some new plastic material would soon eliminate cork as a sealing material
- That, to break its dependence on royalty payments to much larger competitors, the company would have to develop its own proprietary technology
- That future growth required the application of modern management techniques of planning and control throughout the company

By the mid-1960s, still operating on a shoestring, the company started commercial production of a PVC-lined crown using its proprietary HC-7 process. (The key technique, a means of metering the molten plastic at high rates of speed and controlling the placement of the severed blob into a moving metal shell, was invented by Enzo Caviglia, a young Chilean chemical engineer who had been recruited to improve quality control.) The acumen of the young management was proved when all manufacture of cork-lined crowns ceased in the early 1970s.

At the same time, the crown market was changing dramatically. Bottlers and brewers were increasingly using cans, which eventually reduced the volume of bottle crowns from a peak of 350 million gross to the current 175 million gross. Most crown manufacturers were forced out of business; only four survived. To the surprise of many experts, the newly renamed H-C Industries of Crawfordsville was one of the four.

The need for additional income spurred still another innovation drive among the H-C people, who now included a brilliant engineer named Sheldon Wilde. It was triggered by a casual remark by a Coca-Cola executive at a bottlers' convention that bottlers needed a device to mark each container during production so they could identify location, batch, and other essential control data at a later date.

After the usual mistakes, wrong turns, and disappointments, H-C offered the Ultra Mark System throughout the world as well as the United States. Thus, the smallest crown manufacturer in the United States established an impressive international presence. Today, a very significant percentage of the crowns manufactured throughout the world are made with the H-C plastic process and H-C equipment.

H-C even turned a by-product of bottle cap production into a profitable item. This was a sheet of metal scrap with holes made by punching out the crown blanks. H-C sold these sheets for use as retaining devices for fiberglass air-conditioning filters. When declining U.S. crown production created a shortage of the air-filter product, H-C cornered the scrap supply of the foreign crown manufacturers, which enabled it to meet the U.S. market demand. (Another talented H-C executive, Hal Mallory, unexpectedly became an international wizard dealer.)

Betting the Company on Plastic

With sales at $10 million, H-C Industries decided on a major and risky proposition: obsoleting billions of metal crowns by replacing them with plastic crowns. (Plastic crowns were felt to have several advantages, including safety—an important factor because of increasingly costly product-liability suits arising from eye injuries caused by metal crowns.)

The concept of an "H-C Composite Plastic Closure" was born

on June 10, 1976. The task of turning the concept into reality was tremendously difficult, because the technology for maintaining carbonation pressure in beer and soda bottles with plastic crowns simply did not exist. For 3 years, H-C people tried, tested, and discarded scores of ideas. Finally, Sheldon Wilde felt comfortable enough with one approach to recommend the construction of a prototype process to make 30 closures per minute. He estimated the cost at $150,000, the time for completion at 8 to 10 months. "Little did we know," said CEO Jim Smith in retrospect. In actuality, the project took millions of dollars and 6 years to complete.

The long, intense, and costly effort required hard work, dedication, and the investment of every penny of profit contributed by the golden goose, mature metal crown sales, which by 1984 had grown to $25 million. Plastic sales of $6 million were still not profitable, and the production equipment was still in the developmental stage, with continual changes in specifications and methods. To continue took courage, guts, and the dedicated willingness to risk profits on an uncertain venture. However, the arduous struggle up the learning curve was lightened by a favorable patent position and additional technological advancements. The new closure was equipped with a unique and effective "tamper evident" band, christened Winglok—a device that became imperative after the Tylenol tampering episode in 1982.

A Big Gamble Pays Off Big

By 1986, H-C had a winner with immense potential. The development was exhilarating to the participants. Despite the long hours, frustrating errors, many disappointments, and years of profitless scrimping, the struggle and process of overcoming ridiculous odds against giant corporations and their research efforts were fun. A small company made a real impact on a global industry.

It was then the right time to consider the many offers made by large competitors and the "endangered species" of metal crown manufacturers. To become the premier world producer of plastic caps, H-C would need a tremendous influx of new capital for new facilities and new operations. When Alcoa made an offer of $1075 per share for the outright purchase of H-C, Jim Smith and his partners accepted. It was a win-win outcome for all concerned. (After the many years of low-budget existence at H-C, a shareholder asked: "Are you sure a decimal point wasn't misplaced in the Alcoa offer?")

Lesson to Be Learned

H-C Industries' extraordinary results—in the face of severely limited physical and fiscal resources—come from seven qualities that both smallies and biggies must develop if they want to stay in the race.

1. A culture of clever, shoestring-type innovation and invention.
2. Early detection of change in the market.
3. Diversification within its own field of experience—that is, developing different materials for the same bottling market.
4. Major risk-taking philosophy, tempered by good controls, attention to detail, and the willingness and ability to make fast changes of direction when mistakes and dead-end streets show up during development.
5. Very little NIH (not invented here) behavior. No ego stubbornness.
6. Dedication to professional management techniques (planning, strategic alternatives, use of computers, personnel policies, operational methods) far beyond the norm for a $25 million manufacturing company.
7. Uncanny ability for selecting, attracting, cultivating, and challenging extraordinarily talented people. It takes something special to keep and motivate such gorillas in Crawfordsville, Indiana, in competition with the perks and glamor of much bigger and richer companies in far more alluring facilities and locations.

PART SIX

Conclusion: Let's Have Action

18 Action Areas

"There is nothing more difficult to take in hand, more perilous to conduct, or more uncertain in its success, than to take the lead in the introduction of a new order of things." NICCOLO MACHIAVELLI

The entire philosophy of strategic management discussed in this book is based on action orientation. Unless there is action, unless something happens, unless somebody does something, all of the ideas and thoughts that have been expressed here are meaningless. While the process must include periods of thoughtful and sometimes tedious analysis, the results must be dynamic and show tangible progress.

Let's summarize and pull together the ways we have discussed in which management must change its approach if it is to cope successfully with today's—and tomorrow's—unpredictable world.

Talent

Larger companies are losing talented people despite an increasing need for their contribution. These companies should rethink their policies on motivation, rewards, incentives, organization, climate, work environment, and promotion if they want to attract and hold on to talent.

Rewards

The reward system must be changed because society is changing and so is the value system. This is the era of individual rather than group reward (not in Japan, however, where the culture shuns individual-performance rewards). Formulas are being abandoned for one-on-one evaluation and cafeteria-style benefit and compensation options. Valuable individuals and superior performers will be far more satisfied by custom-made solutions than by "canned" compensation.

Delegation/Participation

The participative concept is essential simply because good performers and talented people will not tolerate a dictatorial management style. The trend to real delegation is accelerated by the era of specialization. Generalists don't have the specific knowledge about a growing number of subjects, and they must delegate decisions to the new breed of technocrats.

Bureaucracy

Cutting red tape must become a major objective of any company. Methods and practices must be streamlined to speed up throughput. In times of faster change, faster distribution, faster saturation, and faster obsolescence, bureaucratic red tape must give way to simplification and common sense. No business is exempt from this advice.

Intrapreneurship

Intrapreneurs are rare birds that every business wants to catch. But the cage cannot be shut after you lure the desired species. An enterprise must be so organized that intrapreneurs can remain, enjoy the environment, and add to their own prosperity and that of the business. A more horizontal organization, fewer reporting levels, more direct communication, and less red tape are essential to prevent the bird from flying the coop.

Loyalty

There is a waning of both employee and customer loyalty—as shown by the big increase in job switching and brand switching. Businesses must choose either to function with less loyalty—by subcontracting personnel and going to private labels—or to allocate more resources to loyalty preservation (new personnel policies and bigger marketing and advertising budgets).

Innovation

Faster obsolescence requires more innovation. Creative ideas need encouragement, investment, and acceptance of risk. Companies should reevaluate their risk-taking levels to determine if the levels are high enough to encourage innovation and make it happen. Analysis of worldwide competition can help.

Productivity

Years ago—and better than anyone else since—Peter Drucker summarized the need for better efforts to make an enterprise more productive: "There are enormous numbers of managers who have retired on the job.... Production is not the application of tools to materials, but logic to work." Better productivity, throughout the organization, is everybody's job and everybody's responsibility. It has been estimated that U.S. business operates at 50 percent of its potential. There must be a way to add at least an extra 10 percent to that dismal figure.

Research and Development

Expenditures for R&D must increase in direct proportion to the overall explosion of technological progress. When both the U.S. government and U.S. industry reduced their research budgets during the 1970s, the rest of the world did not—and we are still paying for our national shortsightedness.

The trend is slowly being reversed. Companies will have to reallocate more dollars to development, pool their resources for joint research, purchase licenses, form joint ventures. All that effort is needed to remain at the leading edge of inevitable technological progress. Those who don't make the effort will just disappear.

Marketing

We need less hoopla, less illusion, more facts, more analysis. In this era of pluralism and segmentation, marketing will have to become more precise, more oriented to the ultimate user. Markets that will grow fast must be penetrated fast. New techniques will be necessary for market research, market testing, and market entry. The changes will affect advertising, promotion, public relations, point-of-sale outlets, and methods of distribution. Fresh thinking will be needed from personnel—the good old tricks with mirrors won't do it.

Long-Term View

Many corporations are obsessed with the quarterly bottom-line profit show and tell. It almost seems as though Wall Street analysts are running the companies. The exploitation of short-term gains to the detriment of the future is weakening many businesses. It leads to reductions in service, preventive maintenance, new capital investment, R&D budgets, and market and customer research. This saps vital energies from the future and obviously weakens the business. "Greed created capitalism, and excessive greed is going to kill it."

Fanatical Dedication

Every business enterprise and its managers should select three key phrases to place on top of the pyramid—whether *quality, customer ser-*

vice, lowest cost, highest personnel morale, or whatever. The three resolutions must permeate the entire organization. Management should inspire an absolutely fanatical dedication to the achievement of these fervent goals. (But, as times change, even the objectives of the fanatical dedication must be reevaluated periodically.)

Adaptive-Reactive Style

Adaptation to change requires a different management style. I call it the *3-F style:* fast, fluid, flexible. *Fast:* Quicker recognition of changing conditions and faster decision making in response. *Fluid:* able to flow with the tide in a smooth, not jerky way. *Flexible:* rejection of rigid policies, absolute rules, heavy, ponderous standard-practice manuals—and acceptance of new conditions, new mores, new behavior, without emotional trauma. Don't adopt a 3-S style: slow, stubborn, and stupid.

Psychological Cost of Change

Managers must understand the dynamics of change and the complexities of effecting change in their organizations. Alvin Toffler wrote: "Man has a limited biological capacity for change. When this capacity is overwhelmed, the capacity is in future shock."

The practical reality is that, in executing plans and programs requiring major changes, the shortest distance between the "before" and "after" points is not a straight line. Implementation must take into account the psychological factors, the effects on people, the natural resistance to change and the unknown, ingrained habits, and the trauma of having one's sense of security upset.

The Japanese *ringi* system of predecision indoctrination of everyone who may be affected is psychologically sound. A good manager must be not only a good planner and a good implementer, but a good psychologist as well. Action plans should clearly anticipate psychological shock and incorporate precise steps on how to handle it. These precautions are usually ignored or pooh-poohed as coddling. That's a big and costly mistake.

Alternatives

A General Electric executive coined the term "banana peel strategy." Any business is bound to slip occasionally because of some unexpected event, and it should be ready with an alternative strategy and a set of corrective actions. Today's planners must precondition the organization to potential negative events. This should be taken not as a doom-and-gloom philosophy, but as the recognition of normal conditions for which one should be prepared.

Management Time

Ideally, top management should allocate 70 percent of its time to managing the future by planning, innovating, strategizing, evaluating alternatives, and preparing for change—and only 30 percent to managing the present, responding to fire alarms, and monitoring current operations. Unfortunately, the ratio is usually less than 10 percent for managing the future and more than 90 percent for managing the present.

Managers will maintain that they can't change that ratio—that there just is not enough time for managing both the present and the future. They'll say: "Let someone else theorize about the future while we provide the hard bucks to pay for those eggheads." Wrong. Line managers must plan—and they must find time to do it.

One way they can do it is by better time management. Managers should record and analyze their daily activities over a 3-week period. Then they should arrange those activities in descending order of importance based on the impact they have on company operations.

Then comes the tough decision. Stop doing the bottom one-third of the tasks listed. Don't do them less, or better, or smarter—cut them out completely. There is no point in doing well that which should not be done in the first place. The time saved this way is extraordinary, and it can be devoted to thinking and planning the future.

Control

"Control" shouldn't be a dirty word. It's still valid, still a must despite the recommended direction toward delegation, participation, horizontal organization, intrapreneurship, self-actualization, trust, and confidence.

It can be sugarcoated and called feedback or monitoring, but it still means control. It's the absolute right and duty of corporate executives to know what's going on in the business in time to correct, change, and improve. More corporations go bankrupt because of lack of control than for any other reason. From Penn-Central's creatively fraudulent accounting, to Rolls-Royce's catastrophic cost overrides, to Wickes' overexpansion, to Baldwin's financial games, to Osborne's new-product miscalculations, it's the same story: costly failures because of late and inadequate feedback about the realities of the situation.

Delegation is a good thing—but it doesn't mean abdication. Executives should keep on top of their businesses by supporting computerization of data and electronic transmittal of accounting and operational information via terminals. Technology has made real-time information possible and practical.

However, this in no way should relieve managers from practicing direct, informal, continuous personal and intense communications with their peers, subordinates, and superiors. Terminals, databases, and modem devices should provide the time for, not replace, face-to-face interchange. Hands-on management is still very much in order.

Priorities

The single most important and effective method of managing an enterprise is to set the right priorities and abide by them. One should develop and cultivate a mind-set that automatically arranges thoughts, events, conclusions, plans, and actions in priority order. That applies to any situation, even a trivial one.

The results provide a double advantage. Decisions are better and crisper because they deal with the crux of the matter. And there is more time to think out the important solutions because the lower-priority items have been postponed or discarded. Some 2000 years ago, Diogenes wrote some advice: "Time is the most valuable thing you can spend."

PART SEVEN

Trigger Point Resources

RESOURCES

Keeping informed on key external factors

The following razor blade reading and reference list has been carefully selected from hundreds of available sources. Obviously, it is not all-inclusive, nor will it serve the specific needs of every business person. It does, however, provide a good cross-section of practical and valuable data covering a broad spectrum of socioeconomic information. It is a basis for starting the razor blade reading process. Refinements, additions, and deletions will come with time and practice.

Journals and Magazines

Daily	*The Wall Street Journal* *The Financial Times of London* (U.S. edition of the finest British paper)
Weekly	*Business Week* *U.S. News & World Report*
Biweekly	*The Economist*
Monthly	*Fortune* *Forbes* *INC*
Quarterly	*Economic Outlook, USA* (University of Michigan)

Statistical Reference

Monthly

Economic Indicators (Council of Economic Advisers)*
Survey of Current Business (U.S. Department of Commerce)*
Business Conditions Digest (U.S. Department of Commerce)*
Monthly Labor Review (U.S. Department of Labor)*
International Financial Statistics—IMF, Washington, DC 20402
OECD Observer & Economic Outlook—OECD Publication Center, 1750 Pennsylvania Ave. NW, Washington, DC 20006

Annually

U.S. Statistical Abstract (U.S. Department of Commerce)*
*Economic Report of the President**
*U.S. (Federal) Budget**

Specialized Material

A Trade and technical publications pertinent to the lines of business of the organization

B Functional publications (personnel, marketing, procurement) relating to the executive's main responsibilities

Selected Bibliography on Planning and Strategic Management Classics (1945–1982)

Ackoff, Russell Lincoln: *A Concept of Corporate Planning,* Wiley-Interscience, New York, 1970. (Covers the total planning process. Introduces an interesting concept of adaptive planning.)

Adler, Lee (ed.): *Plotting Marketing Strategy,* Simon & Schuster, New York, 1967. (Discussion of impacts on the market/product interface by the use of various market-directed strategies.)

Allio, Robert J., and Malcolm W. Pennington (eds.): *Corporate Planning: Techniques and Applications,* AMACOM, New York, 1979. (Collection of practical articles from *Planning Review.* Good sounding board for comparison of practices.)

*U.S. government publications are available from the Superintendent of Documents, Government Printing Office, Washington, DC 20402.

Batten, J. D.: *Tough-Minded Management,* AMACOM, New York, 1963. (Down-to-earth, tough approach to management; applicable to today's environment.)

Cannon, J. Thomas: *Business Strategy and Policy,* Harcourt, Brace & World, New York, 1968. (A list of major strategic moves at the corporate and functional levels.)

Channon, Derek F., with Michael Jalland: *Multinational Strategic Planning,* AMACOM, New York, 1978. (Useful review of processes used for multinational operations.)

Christopher, W. F.: *The Achieving Enterprise,* AMACOM, New York, 1974. (Many good suggestions for goal setting and achievement. Good balance of present and future.)

Drucker, Peter F.: *The Practice of Management,* Harper & Row, New York, 1954. (Drucker remains the guru of modern management. His 26-year old classic is still valid, topical, and exciting.)

———: *Management—Tasks, Responsibilities, Practices,* Harper & Row, New York, 1974. (Thorough analysis of management tasks, organization, and strategies. Good reference material.)

———: *Toward the Next Economics and Other Essays,* Harper & Row, New York, 1981. (Peter Drucker is unique. All of his writings contain real gems of true wisdom.)

Henderson, Bruce D.: *Henderson on Corporate Strategy,* Abt Books, Cambridge, Mass., 1979. (Provocative essays representing the philosophy of The Boston Consulting Group.)

Kastens, Merritt L.: *Long Range Planning for Your Business: An Operating Manual,* AMACOM, New York, 1976. (Step-by-step program to implement planning on daily basis, combined with good examples.)

Louden, J. Keith: *Making It Happen,* AMACOM, New York, 1971. (Suggestions on improvement of commitment to objectives by managers at various levels of the organization.)

McGregor, Douglas: *The Human Side of Enterprise,* McGraw-Hill, New York, 1960. (Still a valid and valuable classic on motivation and people management—the X & Y concept.)

Odiorne, George S.: *MBO II,* Pitman, Belmont, Calif., 1979. (MBO has become a "household" word for management by objectives. Odiorne updates his system to adapt to today's conditions.)

Ohmae, Kenichi: *The Mind of the Strategist,* McGraw-Hill, New York, 1982. (Another practical coverage of the Japanese business thinking by a Japanese consultant.)

Ouchi, William G.: *The Theory Z,* Addison-Wesley, Reading, Mass., 1981. (Best seller. Good outline of key philosophical differences between U.S. and Japanese management styles. Good examples.)

Pascale, Richard Tanner, and Anthony G. Athos: *The Art of Japanese Management,* Simon & Schuster, New York, 1981. (Very useful book for better understanding of Japanese management techniques and philosophy.)

Peters, T. J., and R. H. Waterman, Jr.: *In Search of Excellence,* Harper & Row, New York, 1982. (Most successful business book in history. Excellent principles, but case histories are already obsolete: many success examples are today's failures.)

Porter, Michael E.: *Competitive Strategy,* Free Press, New York, 1980. (Techniques for recognizing and dealing with competition. Interesting, market-oriented approach.)

Ross, J., and M. J. Kami: *Corporate Management in Crisis: Why Do the Mighty Fall?* Prentice-Hall, Englewood Cliffs, N.J., 1973. (Case studies of strategic failures and successes. Out of print, but available at libraries.)

Rothschild, William: *Strategic Alternatives,* AMACOM, New York, 1979. (Description and discussion of 37 different business strategies. Good base for comparison.)

Steiner, George A.: *Top Management Planning,* Macmillan, New York, 1969. (The planning "bible" of procedures and techniques. Usually used for reference.)

———: *Strategic Planning,* Free Press, New York, 1979. (Serious analysis of concepts and practices of strategic planning.)

Stonich, Paul J.: *Zero-Based Planning and Budgeting: Improved Cost Control and Resource Allocation,* Dow Jones–Irwin, Homewood, Ill., 1977. (Practical description of ZBB combining step-by-step approach with real examples.)

Warren, E. Kirby: *Long Range Planning—The Executive Viewpoint,* Prentice-Hall, Englewood Cliffs, N.J., 1966. (Solid 90 pages of practical considerations still valid today.)

Selected Bibliography on Planning and Strategic Management New Publications (1983–1987)

Christopher, Robert C.: *The Japanese Mind: The Goliath Explained,* Linden Press, New York, 1983. (Excellent study of the complex Japanese society.)

Clifford, Jr., D. K., and R. E. Cavanagh: *The Winning Performance,* Bantam Books, New York, 1985. (ABC survey of success factors of America's high-growth midsize companies.)

Cook, James R.: *The Start-up Entrepreneur*, E.P. Dutton, New York 1987. (Attacks the myth that entrepreneurs can start a business but cannot manage it.)

De Bono, Edward: *Tactics: The Art and Science of Success,* Little Brown, Boston, 1984. (Analysis of qualities of successful leaders and CEOs.)

Donnelly, Robert M.: *Guidebook to Planning,* Van Nostrand Reinhold, New York, 1984. (Short planning guide for smaller firms.)

Drucker, Peter: *Innovation and Entrepreneurship: Practice and Principles,* Harper & Row, New York, 1985. (Twenty-second book by Drucker has new ideas and fits with the new times and the need for greater innovation.)

———: *The Frontiers of Management,* Dutton, New York, 1986. (Thirty-five essays arranged in logical sequence.)

Edwardes, Michael: *Back from the Brink,* Collins, London, 1983. (Excellent analysis of rebirth of British Leyland. Close parallel to Chrysler.)

Geneen, Harold: *Managing,* Doubleday, Garden City, N.Y., 1984. (Geneen's post-facto thoughts on how he should have managed ITT, not how he actually did.)

Grove, Andrew S.: *High Output Management,* Random House, New York, 1983. (Managerial productivity increase methods by president of Intel.)

Harmon, F. G., and G. Jacobs: *The Vital Difference,* AMACOM, New York, 1985. (Insightful analysis of success factors and case studies.)

Horton, Thomas R.: *"What Works for Me,"* Random House, New York, 1986. (Interviews with 16 CEOs about their careers and commitments.)

Iacocca, Lee: *Iacocca: An Autobiography,* Bantam Books, New York, 1984. (Fascinating combination of personal ambition and business acumen.)

Imai, Masaaki: *Kaizen, The Key to Japan's Competitive Success*, Random House, New York, 1986. (*Kaizen* means "gradual, unending improvement." This book describes 16 *kaizen* practices Western managers can put to work.)

James, Barrie G.: *Business Wargames,* Abacus Press, Cambridge, Mass., 1985. (Interesting analogy between business and military strategies.)

Kanter, Rosabeth Moss: *The Change Masters,* Simon & Schuster, New York, 1983. (Innovating for productivity in American corporations.)

Kastens, Merritt L.: *Maintaining Momentum in Long Range Planning,* AMACOM, New York, 1984. (Methods to step back and look critically at long-range-planning results.)

Keidel, Robert W.: *Game Plans,* Dutton, New York, 1986. (Intriguing comparison of business organizations with sports teams.)

Kotler, P., L. Fahey, and S. Jatusripitak: *The New Competition,* Prentice-Hall, Englewood Cliffs, N.J., 1985. (Analysis of Japanese competitive strategies.)

Kuhn, Robert L.: *To Flourish Among Giants: Creative Management for Mid-Sized Firms,* Wiley, New York, 1985. (Success factors for smaller companies.)

Lamb, Robert Boyden: *Running American Business*, Basic Books, New York, 1987. (Explores the great successes and equally great failures of major U.S. corporations and their CEOs.)

——— (ed.): *Competitive Strategic Management,* Prentice-Hall, Englewood Cliffs, N.J., 1984. (Good selection of articles on strategic analysis.)

LeBoeuf, Michael: *The Greatest Management Principle in the World,* Putnam, New York, 1985. (Pithy methods for rewards and incentives.)

Levinson, H., and S. Rosenthal: *CEO: Corporate Leadership in Action,* Basic Books, New York, 1984. (Interviews with six leaders of major corporations.)

McKenna, Regis: *The Regis Touch,* Addison-Wesley, Reading, Mass., 1985. (Marketing strategies geared to the new times.)

Mills, D. Quinn: *The New Competitors,* Wiley, New York, 1985. (A report on the "new school" of American managers.)

Naisbitt, J., and P. Aburdene: *Re-Inventing the Corporation,* Warner Books, New York, 1985. (No match to *Megatrends.* Popular because of author, not content.)

O'Toole, James: *Vanguard Management: Redesigning the Corporate Future,* Doubleday, New York, 1985. (Case studies and analysis of eight successful companies.)

Peacock, William E.: *Corporate Combat,* Facts on File Publications, New York, 1984. (Another comparison of military vs. business cases.)

Peters, Tom: *Thriving on Chaos*, Alfred A. Knopf, New York, 1987. (Says perpetual change is here to stay and tells why we must learn to live with it.)

Pinchot III, Gifford: *Intrapreuneuring,* Harper & Row, New York, 1985. (How to foment entrepreneurship within a larger enterprise.)

Porter, Michael E.: *Competitive Advantage,* Free Press, New York, 1985. (Good but complex analysis of various business strategies.)

Reich, Robert B.: *The Next American Frontier,* Times Books, New York, 1983. (An important analysis of our changing American socioeconomic culture.)

Rodgers, F. G. "Buck": *The IBM Way,* Harper & Row, New York, 1986. (Insights into IBM's policies and methods of managing.)

Steiner, George A.: *The New CEO,* Macmillan, New York, 1983. (Short descriptions of new characteristics and performance required of a modern CEO.)

Townsend, Robert: *Further up the Organization,* Alfred A. Knopf, New York, 1984. (Witty update of his 1970 classic.)

Waitley, Denis E., and Robert B. Tucker: *Winning the Innovation Game,* Revell, Old Tappan, N.J., 1986. (Practical, pithy approach to innovation and innovators.)

Walton, Mary: *The Deming Management Method,* Dodd, Mead, New York, 1986. (Deming's Japanese success geared to American industry. Excellent.)

Waterman, Robert H: *The Renewal Factor: How the Best Get and Keep the Competitive Edge*, Bantam Books, New York, 1987. (Organziations that have turned themselves around successfully.)

Index

About the Author

Since the 1950s, when he helped pioneer IBM's first strategic planning program, *Michael J. Kami* has been telling companies what to do to stay in business. Now a highly acclaimed consultant and the publisher of the *Kami Strategic Assumptions* newsletter, Kami has been featured on the cover of *Forbes* magazine and is the author of three other books on successful management tactics. Reared in Brazil and Switzerland, Kami received degrees in electrical engineering, business administration, and education from MIT and Florida Atlantic University.